SHE SHALL BE CALLED WOMAN

VOLUME
I

SHE SHALL BE CALLED WOMAN

VOLUME I

OLD TESTAMENT WOMEN

Edited by
Sheila Jones and Linda Brumley

Discipleship

PUBLICATIONS INTERNATIONAL

One Merrill Street
Woburn, MA 01801
1-800-727-8273   Fax (617) 937-3889

She Shall Be Called Woman
Volume I—Old Testament Women
©1994 by Discipleship Publications International
One Merrill Street, Woburn, MA 01801

Cover and layout design: Nora Robbins

Printed in the United States of America

ISBN 1-884553-24-9

DEDICATION

To Our Mothers

Edith DeLano Presley

Ada Louise Parks Tucker

Thank you for teaching us to
love God and his word.

CONTENTS

INTRODUCTION

"You've come a long way, baby!" That's the message our culture is sending to women at the dawn of the 21st century. Frustrated by inequities and undervaluations, women have created new definitions of themselves—definitions born and bred in humanism and self-projection. But how far have women really come and how fulfilled will they be by the new definitions?

The one who made woman is the only one who can define her. God created woman. Then throughout the pages of his Scriptures he unfolded both who he meant for her to be and who she became. Here we find the good, the best, the bad, the worst—a composite to teach us about the gift of our womanhood—a gift which can be used or misused, can motivate or manipulate, can enthrall or ensnare. It boils down to a choice that all women must make—from *garden* century to 21st century. Our way or his way.

Paul tells us that "...everything that was written in the past was written to teach us, so that through endurance and the encouragement of the Scriptures we might have hope" (Romans 15:5). That means that God specifically and strategically placed in the Scriptures the record of every woman from which he wanted us to learn—godly and ungodly. In each we see some of ourselves. In each we see the consequence of a choice—from the evil heart of Jezebel to the servant heart of Ruth.

In the pages of this book we will wrestle with the Scriptures, not letting go until we have been blessed to understand why God told us about each of these sisters of ours. After being encouraged to "live with her woman" for a full month before writing the final response, each writer has grappled with her part of this composite woman. She has been revealed to us over the centuries by the God who wants desperately to teach us how to be *his* woman.

In the following pages you will come to know not only the women of the Old Testament, but the modern women who wrote about them. Each of the writers pours out her heart—honestly, sometimes painfully, but always faithfully. Like the Psalms of David, these readings contain candid, uncensored admissions of need and a grateful, joyful acceptance of grace.

Just like their sisters of old, our writers are women who have lost husbands, who have been sexually abused, who have seen their own faithlessness in response to difficult circumstances. They are real women. They struggle with pride and self-pity. But they are women who have decided that Jesus Christ is their life and their salvation. They fervently believe that dying to self brings about the power and forgiveness of God. And they live what they believe.

Your heart will be touched and stretched. Get ready to laugh, to cry, to be encouraged, to be convicted, to be inspired. Get ready to see yourself and to repent. Get ready to be forever changed by these women of long ago and your contemporaries on their journeys of faith.

Fulfill Isaiah 55:11, vowing that his word will not return to him void. With honesty and humility confront the Scriptures and yourself. Trust in his grace to transform your inner self, to take on the "unfading beauty of a gentle and quiet spirit, which is of great worth in God's sight" (1 Peter 3:4). Trust his grace to transform you into *his* woman. The woman you were meant to be.

Sheila Jones
July 1994

BEFORE YOU START

◆ Each chapter is divided into five sections:

1. Scripture reference
2. Historical background (written by the editors)
3. Character study
4. Writer's personal response
5. Focus question

◆ The chapters were written assuming that you will have read the scripture references *first*. As tempting as it is to skip over them and jump into the meat of the chapter, don't give in! **Read the scriptures first.** We promise you the text will have infinitely more meaning if you do.

◆ To help you apply what you are reading we have included an "Application" section in the back of the book with specific questions to ask after each chapter. Be prepared to see yourself in the mirror of the Word.

1. As you make personal application, you can write a brief response in the space given. Boil it down to a one- or two-sentence insight or commitment. The more simple your response, the better your grasp of what God wanted you to understand.

2. These application questions can also be used in small group discipling situations. It is encouraging and unifying to read and discuss the chapters along with others. We learn more about our character when we are open to others' input. Also, we grow more in our character when we are open to others' support.

1

EVE

Genesis 2, 3, 4; 2 Corinthians 11:3; 1 Timothy 2:13

Eve's history in a word is God. A split second before the world came into being, there was God—God with an idea that only he could bring to fruition. A world with color. Design. Detail. Incredibly delicate balances. And in the middle of it all, man and woman—made to be the objects of his love, to be the reflection of his nature, to be the recipients of his care. The Divine fashioned and then held the hand of mankind. Now mankind must decide if he and she will be led or will let loose.◆

The Garden of Eden. Perfection. Unspeakable beauty. The presence of God. Can you imagine it? Unbroken union with the Creator! Walking with him, talking with him, learning from him, loving and being loved by him! The God who created Adam and Eve in perfection built into them the capacity for choice. Without the power to choose, there would have been no relationship. They would have been nothing more than robots. But if they chose to love God, chose to trust him, chose to obey him, they would hold on to perfection. God made choice viable by placing a forbidden tree in the garden and giving them the option of trust or doubt, obedience or rebellion. With choice came the possibility of deception.

We can better understand how sin's deception works in our lives if we understand how Satan deceived Eve. To look at Eve is to see ourselves. God has a continuing concern for his people in every century: "...I am afraid that just as Eve was deceived by the serpent's cunning, your minds may somehow be led astray from your sincere and pure devotion to Christ" (2 Corinthians 11:3-4). How did Satan lead Eve astray?

The Deception of Doubt

Eve had never seen anything but perfection. Unblemished goodness enveloped and permeated her life. There had been no negative circumstances to cause her to doubt or question God. His goodness, faithfulness, power and love had been shown in every way. She had never been given one reason to suspect that God would withhold anything wonderful from her. She had never experienced sickness, pain, grief, betrayal, war or natural calamity. She had never had an unmet need, a sleepless night or an unanswered prayer. Yet, at Satan's first suggestion that God lacked integrity toward her, Eve entertained doubts!

>Maybe I am missing something heady and intriguing.
>Maybe God is selfishly hoarding a blessing I would really enjoy.
>Maybe he didn't *really* mean what he said.
>Maybe he makes idle threats.
>Maybe he doesn't really have my best interest at heart.

We tend to feel that life's negative circumstances justify our questioning God's benevolence towards us. We get angry at God. Eve's story reveals that it is not our circumstances that make us question God—it is the sinful nature. That is why people with pure hearts grow closer to God in adversity, and those with doubting hearts turn away from God.

The Deception of Desire

The lusts of her flesh blocked her reason. Satan convinced her that she could fulfill her desires and suffer no consequences. *"You will surely not die."* It looked good. It smelled good. It tasted good. It sounded good. She was afraid to miss out. She was curious, restless, feeling unfulfilled. She would be the exception. She would get away with it. Just this one time. Like us: I won't get pregnant. I won't get a sexually transmitted disease, suffer the addiction, the overdose, the breakdown. I won't be charged with drunk driving. Those things happen to other people.

When we are ungrateful for what we do have, we desire what we should not have. The fruit—Eve wanted its beauty, flavor and power. She wanted the knowledge of good and evil. She already had the knowledge of good; for the first, last and only time in history, human beings experienced perfect good! But she was not able to appreciate it until she had experienced evil, and then it was too late—for all of us!

What must this grieving mother have thought as she stood weeping over the grave of her son, Abel, who was senselessly murdered by his brother, Cain, knowing that she had wanted the knowledge of good and evil? In essence, she had asked to witness this shameful horror! Satan must have been delighted. *You want to see evil? I will show you evil!* And with the permission of our own sinfully curious natures, Satan continues to show us evil—tragic, chaotic, destructive evil.

The Deception of Distance

I wonder where Eve thought God was while she carried on this little chat with Satan and wiped the fruit juice off her chin with the back of her hand? She was like the prodigal son who "set off for a distant country" and there squandered his wealth in wild living. In senseless denial, Eve distanced herself from an all-seeing God. Then upon hearing him approach, she pathetically attempted to hide.

We distance ourselves with self-deception. God appeals to us not to kid ourselves about sin and its consequences (Galatians 6:7-8; James 1:16-17, 22-27). What lies did Eve tell herself to blur the clarity of God's instructions: "You are free to eat from any tree in the garden; but you must not eat from the tree of the knowledge of good and evil, for when you eat of it you will surely die" (Genesis 2:16-17)? We feel insulted when we become victims of someone else's lies—how much more insulting it is to become victims of our lies to ourselves! That's what happens when mind games shut out reality. Fantasy convinces us that everything will be all right in spite of our sin. We misinterpret God's grace to mean that he will sweep sin under the rug (Romans 6).

We distance ourselves not only from the reality of God's presence, but also from his clear and perfect standard. We back away from that standard as we interpret, rationalize, minimize and blameshift. Eve used all of these techniques when she answered God's question. *"What is this that you have done?"* he asked. Her rationalized, minimized, blameshifted response was, *"The serpent deceived me and I ate."*

We cannot slip things past God. But our natures long to believe the deception that a sin is too small, too brief, too unavoidable or too long ago for God to have noticed or remembered. And, just as he asked Eve, God asks us, "Where are you?" He asks, not because he does not know, but because he wants to give us an opportunity to admit where we are and to come back to him.

Grateful or Doubtful?

Like Eve's, my life is filled with evidence of God's faithfulness, but by nature I am not a grateful person. Although I have grown to be more focused on solutions than on problems, I still sometimes fail the tests and give way to worry or doubt.

Last summer, our youngest son, Matt (20 years old and a college junior), left Chicago for Syracuse, New York, to be part of a new church. He was full of dreams to do great things for God. There were blessings on every hand: he loved the church, his friends, his classes and his job. But there was something in the air in Syracuse that caused Matt to have daily asthma attacks. By September his condition was life-threatening. Prolonged, acute coughing had perforated both his lungs. In October he finally realized he would have to leave in order to get well.

Satan was right there, urging me to be faithless and fearful. He whispered, sometimes shouted, doubt-provoking questions in my ears:

Maybe he never should have gone to Syracuse in the first place.
Maybe irreparable damage has been done to his lungs and he'll be
    sickly for the rest of his life.
What an expensive waste to have to drop his classes mid-semester!
What if he gets discouraged about losing a year and doesn't go back
    to school?
Why would God give him the best friends, job and classes he's ever had
    and then take it away so quickly?
Why this?
Why that?
Why something else?
I have a right to worry. After all, I *am* his mother.

Stop it, Satan!

When I stayed in touch with my profound gratitude to God for his faithfulness to Matt throughout his life, for the people God had surrounded him with, for the lessons that are only learned through trials, I was able to gain perspective. There was no reason to believe that God would suddenly stop blessing and directing Matt's life or that this illness was an interruption to God's plan. Hope. Peace. Joyful expectation. What's next, Father?

Matt has just moved to Los Angeles, healthy, happy, eager to get back into school, spiritually growing and challenged. God has proven his faithfulness in this new situation now that Matt has relocated. My constant challenge in the face of trials is to refuse to entertain doubts. Staying focused on the abundant evidence of God's love and faithfulness is what will keep me deaf to the doubts Satan lays before me—and worry *is* doubt.

When Eve became ungrateful for what she had, she was easy prey for the deception of doubt. We tend to take for granted whatever blessings we are used to, even perfection, if we have nothing with which to compare it! Gratitude is the essential element of living a faithful, doubt-free life!

Linda Brumley
Elmhurst, Illinois

FOCUS

What problems tempt you to lose a grateful focus on God's blessings in your life and cause you to worry or doubt?
Do you spend more time focused on problems or solutions, fears or faith?

2

SARAH

**Genesis 11:27-32, 12, 15, 16, 17, 18:1-15, 20, 21, 23;
Galatians 4:21-25; Hebrews 11:11-14**

Before God revealed his will to his people by the written word, the first instance being to Moses on Mt. Sinai, he revealed himself and his will through verbal communication. He chose certain men to actually hear his voice, or he sent heavenly messengers in human form to speak for him. The men who heard the voice of God and then passed his message along to their clans are referred to as patriarchs. The Bible does not indicate how God chose the men to whom he gave this privilege and responsibility, but they were rightly regarded with special honor.

The most prominent patriarch of all was Abram (Abraham). He and Sarai (Sarah) were wealthy and settled. But when Abram was 75 years old, God spoke to him and told him to leave all that comfort to spend the rest of his life living in tents, moving from one location to another in the land of Canaan. This order from God was based on three promises: that the old and childless couple would produce offspring to outnumber the stars; that these descendants would one day possess the land in which they had lived as aliens; and that one day not just the Hebrew nation, but every nation on earth would be blessed through a Messiah born into that family.♦

"Sarai was barren." The Bible begins her story with these three words (Genesis 11:30). From such an inauspicious beginning, she went on to encounter adventures, challenges, difficulties and blessings, and ended up being a most honored woman of God, "the mother of all nations" (Genesis 17:16). Her life consisted of 123 years of learning, the last 50 being especially full and rewarding. She changed so radically during the course of her life that God felt only a name change could do her justice: Sarai became *Sarah*, meaning *princess*.

"Go to the Land I Will Show You"

Sorting, organizing provisions, instructing servants; packing boxes for the family, provisions for the servants, grain for the

*animals, utensils for cooking, tents and blankets for the cold
nights under the stars. At last the bags are loaded, tearful good-
byes and longing hugs are exchanged for the last time. The camel,
sheep and human mob set off through the desert. With one last
glimpse, a chapter of her life is closed and a new one opened.*

Sarah's first act of faith was to leave her family and home and set out
for a strange place. As challenging as travelling is in our day and time,
it was even more so then. For Sarah it meant not only packing needed
clothing, but moving the entire household. They had to move themselves,
servants, family and supplies for all. Unlike our moving from one house
to another and settling in, they were constantly on the move, carrying their
"house" with them. God's command in Genesis 12 was for them to go to
an *unknown* place. This had been tried before! Abraham's own father
Terah had *started* for Canaan but never finished, settling down in Haran
before he got to Canaan (Genesis 11:27-32).

How easy it is to want to settle down somewhere spiritually! We start
off committed and sacrificial, yet perhaps find ourselves looking for and
settling for a comfortable spot. This is not a reflection of age or lifestyle,
but a reflection of attitude. Abraham and Sarah re-started their travels
for God at 75, a middle-age time for them—a time when most of us are
putting down roots and pushing up daisies. Incredibly, their traveling
continued for 50 years! Settling once near Sodom and Gomorrah and
continuing through Egypt, they finally reached their destination, only to
stay on the move within Canaan too.

Show Your Love

*Casting a last longing glance at her brother, a beautiful woman
contritely bows her head and, with a heart full of love, walks
forward to face a new challenge. Her steps slow as she enters the
chamber. Seated on the throne is a stranger, now to be her new
master—a master who could protect and honor her brother and
make life easier for him. Harder for her, but better for her brother.*

Sarah's marriage to Abraham could certainly never be categorized as
easy. Constant moving, infertility, extramarital relationships, lying and
family conflicts were but a few of the challenges they faced and overcame.
No wonder God holds Sarah up as the *prime* example of submission and
support for her husband—the example each of us is to imitate (1 Peter 3:1-6).

Because of Sarah's great beauty, Abraham asked her to identify herself as his sister—a deceptive, though true statement (Genesis 20:12). This was helpful for Abraham's safety, but it could only have been unbearable for Sarah. She was taken by Pharaoh as his wife (Genesis 12:19). Abraham was treated well for her sake, and in the end God took care of Sarah. As they left Egypt, Abraham had indeed been blessed. He had his wife back and was a much richer man.

(Since the law had not yet been given and sin not yet been defined, Sarah did not violate God's law by obeying her husband. Certainly, as Christians, we should never go against God's law in order to please our husbands or anyone else. But we do need to imitate the submissive heart of Sarah.)

A similar situation occurred with Abimelech. Sarah again was willing to put herself at risk to help Abraham. He even posed the deception to her as a way of showing her love for him (Genesis 20:13). Sarah was submissive to Abraham, but it must have been difficult, even terrifying, for her.

A friend once defined submission for me as putting someone else's needs ahead of your own. This definition has stuck with me through the years as it puts the meaning of submission into proper perspective: It is a matter of roles, of working together as a team, and of practically implementing Philippians 2—considering others first. This is what Sarah did. She put Abraham's needs and desires first, not her own. God honored Sarah's submission and met her needs by protecting her from Abimelech. Be assured that God is *always* in control and will watch over us and meet *our* needs when we put others' needs first.

Sarah proved to Abraham how much she loved him. She showed it by her attitude and by the degree to which she was willing to please him. That is certainly a standard that challenges most of us modern, equal-rights, equal-pay, equal-everything women. Sarah didn't worry about equality and fairness. She was concerned with loving Abraham and meeting his needs.

I'll Do It My Way

The rod in her hand twitches and trembles as she brings it down on her worthless lazy servant. "You should work harder. Being with child is no excuse for not working. Get back to work and do something!" Turning away, she wipes the jealous tears from her eyes with a weary hand and tosses the stick to the floor. Dejectedly she looks out of the tent at the land before her and wonders if she will ever have offspring who will see it.

Sarah knew Abraham was to have an heir. After so many years of barrenness, the futility of trying, the months and months of disappointment, the years of longing, she finally reasoned that it was not to be through her. She thrust her servant into Abraham's arms and bitterly awaited the outcome.

After the scenario went according to her plan, she couldn't stand it. Frustrated with her body, her servant and her husband, she exploded with rage, unleashing venom on poor Hagar and Abraham.

Sarah, through her own impatience, frustration and worldly thought had made her own problems. It was not God's fault or Abraham's. How carelessly she blamed her husband: "You are responsible for the wrong I am suffering" (Genesis 16:5).

Like Sarah we all must fight the temptation to force things to work out according to our plans. Sarah learned a lesson the hard and painful way: Forcing is fruitless; waiting patiently has far better results.

God Has Brought Me Laughter

Her breath coming in short gasps, she utters one last cry and falls back in exhaustion. The babe is placed in her arms, and gazing down into a small red face, she laughs with joy. Isaac, the long-awaited, much-hoped-for, unbelievable promise, was lying in her arms. Squeezing him to her she laughs and cries with tears of gratitude to a God who could truly do anything.

Sarah talked to God's angel face to face. Unfortunately, she also had the audacity to doubt and question the angel. When God told her that in one year she would have a son, she laughed (scoffed) then tried to deny her reaction. God gave her a promise, and she doubted.

So often we doubt and deny the promises that God is giving us. For Sarah the time wasn't right. For us it's often too soon, too late, too much or not enough of whatever it is we want or think we need. The truth is, just as God was trying to bless Sarah, he is also wanting to bless us. Like Sarah, we often see only the difficulties and delays, but we need to keep God's perspective—nothing is too hard for him (Genesis 18:14).

God did not condemn Sarah for her doubts; he just built her faith. One year later Isaac was born, and Sarah's life was indeed filled with laughter.

Sarah realized Isaac was a blessing from God and shared that joy with others. She knew Isaac was the child of promise and could inspire others to know God (21:1).

Mother of Us All

Head bowed, eyes red, his heart now cut in half and so heavy as he lays his beautiful wife in the best tomb all his riches could buy—still not enough to honor her. It is such agony to leave her as his journey continues. Abraham mourns the loss of Sarah, his spiritual partner. She had been with him through tough times, weaknesses, insecurities, doubts and fears. Now he is alone.

Sarah died at the age of 123 and was buried in Canaan. She had set out to go to God's promised land and never stopped until she got there. She did not influence Abraham to stop, or try to hold him back. Hebrews 11 applauds both Abraham and Sarah for being people of vision and for looking ahead, not back (vss 15-16). Instead of always looking at what she had left, Sarah kept looking forward to all the blessings of being with God. Her wanderings were over. Sarah stayed committed to God and his plan—even to her last breath.

For every father in the world somewhere there is a mother as well. So when God gave Abraham the promise to be the father of many nations, it logically follows that Sarah would be the mother. But it was not simply an assumed role by virtue of association: God specifically wanted Sarah to be the mother of all nations (Genesis 17:16). Such a promise was fulfilled to a woman who was elderly, feisty, often impetuous, sometimes spiteful, but most of all, *faithful.* She had moved wherever God had told her to go. She was willing to be used by God. She was hospitable. She made mistakes but kept growing in her faith. More than anything—**she never quit.**

Such a woman God was proud to hold up to all as a great example (1 Peter 3:4-6). She was to be the matriarch for kings and conquerors. But what about us? Spiritually, is she our mother? Have we embraced and imitated her life and example?

A Righteous Act to Follow

Incredulous, amazed, overwhelmed, inspired, convicted, challenged, hopeful: These are the various feelings that have assailed me as I have "lived with" Sarah.

I know Sarah had weaknesses and sins, but as I look at the big picture of her life I am truly amazed. The degree to which she kept giving and going is intimidating. I realize I must keep going and growing in my commitment to God. We have moved eight times in our 10 years of marriage and lived on both sides of the U. S. and of the Pacific. New food, cultures, language and people are what Sarah encountered as well; and yet, she kept her focus on obeying God. She was 75 and I am half her age. I guess I have a long way to go to catch up and keep up with her.

I am challenged by her submissiveness. It humbles me to see how much she trusted God and Abraham. If frightens me to see the degree to which I must change and be more submissive to Scott. Truly 90% of our conflicts would vanish if I could quit giving way to fear. Fear of mistakes. Fear of life not being fair. Fear of not being heard. *Give it up,* I say. I need not to be frightened to change, but to give up the fear of losing myself and submit! God always took care of Sarah; he will take care of me as well.

She was deeply in love with Abraham and he with her. I am amazed by the demonstration of her love by becoming another man's wife (for a short time as it turned out, but originally she did not know that). That depth of love and sacrifice is painful to me. She truly loved Abraham enough to do what he wanted, even in a moment of his weakness. She did it not once, but twice! So often I see in myself impatience and an expectation for *others* to be perfect. I see an attitude of "I may forgive you once, but you better not do it again!" Sarah kept obeying Abraham without incriminating and badgering him.

I realize, after 10 years of marriage, that it takes work to maintain a relationship of deep, committed love. Sarah and Abraham had to go through tough times, but they emerged victorious and closer than ever. They give me a vision of the kind of relationship for which Scott and I need always to strive.

God commends Sarah and calls me to be her daughter. I pray and strive to have the kind of life, love, marriage and courage that will make God, my Father, proud today! Truly a tough, but righteous, act to follow.

Lynne Green
Hong Kong

 Do you believe that God will be true to his promises to you? Do you trust that he will work his will in your life, or do you try to make things happen according to your script?

3

HAGAR

TRUSTING GOD WHEN LIFE ISN'T FAIR

Genesis 16, 21:1-21; Galatians 4:21-31

Early in Abraham and Sarah's journeys through the land of Canaan, a famine forced them to travel to Egypt. During their stay, the wealthy Abraham became even more wealthy, acquiring many more animals and slaves. Sarah acquired Egyptian maidservants, among them a young woman named Hagar. The famine passed, and they left Egypt with their vast possessions and returned to wandering through Canaan.◆

Hagar's dark eyes shifted uncomfortably as she had another late-night talk with her mistress, Sarah, who trusted Hagar and confided in her. This night, as with so many nights before, there were tears as Sarah shared her struggle with her inability to conceive a child.

Sarah's love for God created in Hagar a desire to know him. It was hard to understand that there was one God over all, especially since she had worshipped many gods in Egypt. But listening to Sarah and Abraham made him seem so real.

Many times Hagar had wished to be like Sarah. She was so confident, so joyful, so beautiful inside and out, so loved by her husband and so respected by her friends. Hagar often watched her and imitated her elegant style.

The Promised Child

In the early years it was fun to be around Sarah as she anxiously awaited the promised child. But as time passed and Sarah began to lose hope, Hagar found it harder to please her mistress. Sarah's scheme to fulfill God's promise came as an incredible challenge to Hagar's heart that night. Although many anxious thoughts raced through her mind, she was excited to think that she could actually bear the promised child.

Both women were surprised, and yet relieved, as Abraham consented to Sarah's plan. In a short time, Hagar was pregnant. Thoughts of her child consumed her. She enjoyed all the attention. Why did Sarah need this child? She, Hagar, was the young, beautiful woman chosen to fulfill a promise. Every time she heard Sarah's joy as she made plans for her child, Hagar stiffened and became withdrawn. Her once-beautiful dark eyes bore the look of contempt and uneasiness when she was in the presence of her mistress.

Insecurity and jealousy gripped Sarah, and she accused her husband of disloyalty. With Abraham's permission, Sarah treated Hagar harshly. Hagar could not believe the sudden turn of events that threatened her new position! She had forgotten who she was, a slave, and desired an exalted position more than she desired to be loyal to her mistress. Instead of begging for forgiveness, Hagar fled. She hated conflict, and besides, in her heart she knew she had been wronged. How could Sarah mistreat her so badly? She had done only as she had been told. Bitterness and resentment invaded and consumed her heart. Maybe she was the hope for the future and not Sarah.

"Go Back and Submit"

An angel met her near a spring on the road to Shur (which means *wall*). She was going to hit an impossible wall in her life unless she dealt with her sin and worked out her conflict with Sarah. God heard her tears—tears of confusion and self-pity—and promised to bless her child! This God of Abraham and Sarah was in control and had seen her suffering! *All* she had to do was go back to Sarah and submit!

Submit! What did that mean? She was used to submitting to Sarah in household chores, but this command coming from God meant so much more. Would Sarah treat her harshly? Would she demand her child? Submitting to God meant submitting to the people he put in authority over her. Now that she believed in God, she had to prove it by trusting him and trusting the people he put in her life.

Her heart raced as she thought about his promise to her—a direct promise from God for her unborn son, Ishmael (*God hears*). "I will so increase your descendants that they will be too numerous to count" (Genesis 16:10). She rejoiced that this promise was as exciting as the one to her master and mistress. But uneasiness struck as she remembered that the angel had said he would be like a wild donkey and that he would live in hostility toward his brothers. *Why was he not going to do something great like the child promised to Abraham and Sarah?* Not knowing how she would be received and pondering these questions in her heart, Hagar started her journey back home.

As the years went by, a warm feeling flowed inside Hagar as she watched her son with his father, Abraham. They enjoyed being together, and she could always find Ishmael at his side.

Hagar gathered her son to her and told him of God's intervention in their lives and how special he, Ishmael, was. As time passed, it seemed to Hagar that her son might be Abraham's only heir. After all, Abraham and Sarah were getting so old. Ishmael began to believe this too and gloried in his position.

The Promise Fulfilled

Ishmael's dark eyes were very much like his mother's. At the birth of Isaac, he looked off in the distance in thoughtful disbelief. As Isaac grew, Ishmael kept his distance as bitterness and resentment burdened his heart. As much as his father tried, he could not create a loving relationship between the two boys. Ishmael mocked and teased his younger brother whenever he could. His brother was taking his place. Hagar did nothing to stop the ridicule, but "understood" his actions deep in her heart.

Then came the most devastating day for Hagar. A day that, deep in her heart, she had feared would come. Abraham asked her and her son to leave his home. How could this be...his oldest son? Hagar's round, dark eyes squinted in distrust and unbelief. Why was he doing this? In Abraham's eyes she saw pain and tears as he embraced his son for the last time and sent them on their way. God had assured him that Ishmael, as his offspring, would be made into a great nation. Abraham again proved faithful in his obedience.

Although Abraham guided them in the right direction, Hagar soon became disoriented and, finally, lost. After all the water and hope were gone, she prepared for them to die. She could not deal with this disheartening dilemma and looked the other way. Tears flowed from their eyes.

In the stillness of the desert, she again heard an angel's voice telling her where to find water. This child of Abraham's was special, and God had heard his tears. Hagar made a home in the desert for herself and her teenage son and later went into her familiar and idolatrous Egypt to find him a wife.

Years later, the Apostle Paul compares Hagar to the old covenant given to Moses on Mt. Sinai. This law gave the people rules to obey, but did not deal with the heart. In the same way, Hagar obeyed Sarah, and then God, but her heart was not with them. She would always be a slave to her own heart sins and would rely constantly on her own human efforts. Ishmael was a result of this human effort and became very much like his mother with the same attitudes and rebellion. Ishmael's descendants lived in hostility toward their Israelite brothers, a hostility which has endured to this very day.

Thank God we have Jesus and the new covenant. We no longer have to be slaves to our heart sins but are free to have an eternal relationship with him.

The Freedom of Submission

"Go back and submit." God often has given me the same direction he gave Hagar. Submission is a scary word. It means someone else is in control.

For most of my life, I was in control, fighting for my "rights." Anger and self-pity dominated my decisions. Like Hagar, I would run from conflict rather than face the difficulty of resolving it.

It was not easy becoming a disciple of Christ, knowing I must submit totally to his word. Oh, I thought I loved God and tried to demonstrate it by the things I did. But, in my heart, scriptures such as Philippians 2:1-11–putting others first, being a servant, being last–revealed my true heart. Like Hagar, I knew what I *should* do, but my heart was not there.

Finally, several years ago, I made a profound discovery. The more of my heart I gave and the more I served, the happier and freer I became. Submitting was allowing myself to be used by God...*his* way.

Submitting does not stop just with God and his word. He expects me to submit to the people he has put in my life to help me. These relationships are among the greatest blessings in the kingdom of God and also among the most challenging. Close relationships require openness, humility and forgiveness. How can I say I love God and not love my sisters from the heart?

God has put some incredible women in my life to help me. At times, I am humble and grateful for the input. At other times, I am prideful and resentful. *But they just don't understand my situation,* I tell myself.

I can understand how Hagar could have felt wronged and unwanted. But her response was to harden her heart. For years she was not open with Sarah, but mechanically did her job as required. She remained a slave in her heart.

No matter how wonderful and spiritual the women are in my life, they cannot help me if they do not know what is going on in my heart. My sinful nature allows me to hear what is said to me through the filter of the question, "Is it fair?" I am also very good, in my sinful nature, at watering down advice if I find sin or fault in the other person's life.

Hagar's story could have had a different ending if she had been humble and submissive. Perhaps the course of her son's life and that of his descendants could have been different.

I am thankful that with God I am not a slave to my sinful nature. I am thankful that the blood of Jesus Christ flows freely throughout my heart to bring forgiveness and change. I must constantly be open to the love and challenge of those around me to keep my heart and my soul in the best spiritual condition.

Sally Hooper
Dallas, Texas

 How eager am I to be submissive toward the leaders in my life? Do I stuff my attitudes or clear them out through openness, honesty and confession?

4

LOT'S WIFE

THE DANGER OF LOOKING BACK

**Genesis 13:1-18, 14:8-16, 18:16-33, 19:1-38;
Luke 17:29-33; 2 Peter 2:6-9**

Lot was Abraham's nephew. They moved to Canaan when Abraham first received his promise and marching orders from God. Both men were wealthy and had vast herds. Conflict sparked between Lot's and Abraham's herdsmen when their herds exceeded the land's capacity to feed them. Abraham, generous and humble, gave Lot first choice of location. They separated when Lot chose the fertile plains of the Jordan near Zoar.

It was desirable land and therefore densely populated, but its moral depravity was so great that the name of the town of Sodom is still synonymous with sexual perversion. God, in a beautiful concession to his friendship with Abraham, delayed destroying Sodom until he had informed him of the plan. Abraham begged for God's mercy and moved God's heart. The final bargain struck between Abraham and God was to spare Sodom if 10 faithful people could be found there. They were not to be found. The destruction would happen on schedule.

Still, a merciful God sent angelic messengers to warn Lot to get out of town. But, even with the messengers' urgent plea, even with a terrifying homosexual rape attempt on that final night, even with the danger to his virgin daughters, Lot hesitated to abandon his home. His wife hesitated even more.◆

L ike many before and after him, Lot was a privileged person. He had great wealth, a rich heritage and endless possibilities for his life. Lot also had a special place in God's heart. God considered him a righteous man and appreciated Lot's distress over the evil lives of the people in Sodom and Gomorrah.

When we are introduced to Lot's wife, she has only a few hours left to her life. Within 24 hours of the angels' visit to Lot's home, the destiny of his wife would be sealed. Along with her family, she was offered a gracious opportunity—to be saved from the destruction coming to all who lived in her town. Why didn't she see it? Why didn't she take it? Why wasn't she saved? Three heart attitudes sealed her fate.

The "Leave Me Alone" Philosophy

She was married to a godly man. "Lot, a righteous man, was distressed by the filthy lives of lawless men" (2 Peter 2:7). How could she be married to Lot and not be a righteous woman? Unfortunately, she did not allow his righteousness to affect or change her.

There is no question that Lot had his faults. He did not have a super strong character. He was greedy (Genesis 13:10-11), made some bad choices (Genesis 13:12-13), was not respected by his future sons-in-law (Genesis 19:14), was hesitant about obeying God (Genesis 19:16), and was manipulated by his daughters (Genesis 19:30-38). Perhaps Lot's wife looked at these weaknesses and thought she had reason to disrespect and disobey and think, *You're no better than I. Just leave me alone, Lot.*

How often are we like Lot's wife? (Maybe her name was "Leave Me Alone.") As wives, we see faults in our husbands' lives and then cannot see the good qualities we need to imitate. Sure, they have faults, but so do we. Just as we want to be respected, we need to respect. If we focus on the mistakes, failures and sins of our husbands, we will never benefit from the strengths, talents and qualities which God sees.

If our husbands are Christians, we must allow them to influence our lives. If they are not Christians, we must watch falling into the self-righteous assumption that they cannot teach us anything. Our husbands know us, and they know how our attitudes and behaviors affect them. We need to listen—both to Christian and non-Christian husbands. In fact, everyone—married or single—needs the influence and input of close *others*. We simply will not grow spiritually in a self-imposed, prideful vacuum.

Love of the World

Peter goes on to say, "...for that righteous man, living among them day after day, was tormented in his righteous soul by the lawless deeds he saw and heard" (2 Peter 2:8).

Lot saw Sodom as God saw it. He felt the same emotions that God felt *(distress, torment)*. Obviously, Lot's wife did not feel these same things. She was attracted to the world and the "things" of the world. When it came down to making a decision, she loved the world more than God.

The pull of the world is very powerful on us women. Clothes, houses and material things appeal to our sinful natures. We spend money we do not have and justify it by saying, "I had to have it." We are required to live in the world, but we must not let the world live in us. Lot's wife left the city, but the city never left her.

Sacrificing for the kingdom is very unnatural. Kingdom-minded women must have a go-anywhere, do-anything, give-up-everything attitude. When called to leave the comforts of a first-world nation, we must not hesitate. When called to move from one city to another for the kingdom's advancement, we must trust and obey. We have lived in five different cities within the last seven years. God has richly blessed our family with every move because of our faith and attitude.

Looking Back

Looking back seems so insignificant, so innocent. She just wanted to see what was happening. Like with Eve—eating a piece of fruit seemed so insignificant, so innocent. She just wanted to have deeper understanding. But when God says, "Do not look back" or "Do not eat of the fruit," he means it. Faith tells us that whatever it is that seems so insignificant, so innocent, is not best for us. Otherwise, God would have told us to do it.

God considered looking back very serious. He specifically commanded the family, "Do not look back." Just as the eating of the fruit revealed Eve's heart, her lack of respect and trust for God, so did the looking back of Lot's wife.

In Luke 9:62 Jesus said, "Anyone who puts his hand to the plow and looks back is not fit for service in the kingdom of God." We are warned not to look back at the world. Falling away does not happen suddenly. Women who fall away begin with looking back to the world. Their looking back seems so insignificant, so innocent. They forget the loneliness, emptiness and grossness of their former life, and they glamorize "the good times."

What we look at determines our standard. We cannot continually look at and think about something without eventually being controlled by it. If we look at the world, it will control us. Lot's wife did not have a deep enough conviction about looking to God, and that lack of conviction destroyed her life.

The Bottom Line

Lot could have helped his wife change her heart if she had allowed it. He saw sin and degradation in the lives of the people. She only saw the luxuries, the pleasures and the false hopes. She foolishly believed that

material things make life worthwhile. She was convin
things her way and in her own time was real life.

When we maintain this philosophy of life we will be in ιυ.
awakening one day. We must see the real issues of life. We must reaι.
what is most important. As Jesus says in Luke 9:24, "Whoever wants
to save his life will lose it, but whoever loses his life for me will save it."

Our possessions, prestige and accomplishments will only deceive us
into thinking we have life. When Lot's wife looked back, she saw that
possessions, prestige and accomplishments turn into ashes. The hard
heart she had cultivated turned her into a lifeless pillar of salt.

There is a point of no return when we look back. We cannot be
prideful, independent, self-sufficient and worldly and expect our hearts
to be righteous when the day of decision comes. We must change our
"Leave Me Alone" philosophy to "Leave Me Not Alone," so that we will
be able to be influenced by the righteous lives of our husbands and
others. Then we will have hearts which are daily sold out to God.
Remember Lot's wife!

Leave Me Not Alone

The leave-me-alone attitude of Lot's wife is one that could easily creep
into my life. As a child I could play by myself for hours. As a teenager
I developed the "if-you-do-not-like-me-I-do-not-need-you" philosophy. In
dating, if someone did not do things my way, I left them. Needless to say,
I have a very strong, independent, self-sufficient nature.

For several years of my life, I focused on my husband's faults and was
not able to benefit from his strengths. As a result, I began to see his
strengths as faults also. I saw his boldness as pushy, his directness as
harsh, and his aggressiveness as insensitive. My pride would not let me
be corrected by him. I would think, *Who do you think you are correcting
me, with all your faults?*

When I finally saw my heart and ungodly attitude, I was able to repent
and see things as they really were. I needed Bruce to help me change
my shyness and cowardice into boldness, my beating-around-the-bush
into directness, and my passiveness into an aggressiveness that could

ιake a great impact on people. Then God started using me in a greater way in the kingdom as we moved to Boston, San Diego, Chicago and then to Los Angeles. I thank God for Bruce who did not leave me alone, had the expectations of God, and helped me become a godly and righteous woman.

I still have to fight that old nature. It tries to raise its ugly head when I am corrected, or if someone does not want to do something my way. Thank God that I now have a heart that can see the destructive nature of a leave-me-alone attitude. I see that without correction I would never change. I see how others' input helps me and how my way is not always the best way. I am thankful for the lesson of Lot's wife, that I must have a leave-me-NOT-alone attitude.

I need others in my life so I will not love the world and depend on "things" for my happiness, security and sense of accomplishment. The material can blind me to the eternal. Here in Los Angeles, God has used fires, floods, riots and earthquakes to remind me of the temporary nature of the material. I am so thankful for my friend and discipler, Elena McKean, because her life and her words help me remember what is really important in life—a daily walk with God, love for the lost, a respectful attitude towards my husband, and a deep devotion to my family. I need Bruce and Elena to help me stay God-focused.

Because of Lot's wife, I have more appreciation for God's hard-line teaching on not looking back. Looking back weakens my faith and character. Looking back is deceptive. I think it has no effect on me, but it keeps me from being able to focus on God and, thus, to grow. If I am not advancing, I am retreating. If I am not looking ahead, I am looking back. By remembering Lot's wife, I am committed to looking *forward* to the ways God will use my life to advance his kingdom.

Robyn Williams
Los Angeles, California

 FOCUS Is your heart totally sold out for God, or are there "things" you hold on to? How often do you look back? Why?

5

REBEKAH

ACCORDING TO HER DESIRES

**Genesis 22:23, 24:1-67, 25:19-34,
26:34-35, 27:1-46, 28:1-9; Romans 9:10**

The entire Bible story can be outlined under the three promises to Abraham:

1. Your descendants will outnumber the stars.
2. Your descendants will possess land inhabited by their enemies.
3. All nations will be blessed through your seed.

The growth of Abraham's family to a mighty nation that would come to "outnumber the stars" begins with detailed accounts of those first families in his lineage: Isaac and his family, Jacob and his family, and Jacob's 12 sons who came to be the fathers of the 12 tribes of Israel. All these stories are recorded in Genesis.

Exodus through Malachi charts the history of that family-expanded-to-nation as they journey from slavery in Egypt to the promised land, and as they conquer and struggle to retain possession of the land. Their possession of the land was dependent on their faithfulness to God.

The New Testament is the story of Abraham's seed, Jesus, through whom not just the nation of Israel, but every nation, would be blessed.

But in those early days of the story, when the players could scarcely foresee the significance of their roles in this unfolding drama, a servant was sent from the aging patriarch's bedside. He swore to return with a wife for Isaac from Abraham's own family and native land. What kind of young woman would agree to leave her family for an unseen land and an unknown man? A woman like Rebekah.◆

"Strong, handsome, successful man in his early 40s looking for a suitable wife from the area of northwest Mesopotamia," the personal ad could have read. Isaac needed a wife. Abraham was determined to keep his son in Canaan, but he was also determined to keep him from marrying any of the Canaanite women. The servant whom Abraham sent to search for the right woman knew he had a difficult task—finding a wife for his master's son without taking Isaac on the journey with him. So, after receiving his instructions, he set out for Nahor, wondering how he would find a suitable woman and if she would come with him once he found her.

No Ordinary Trip to the Well

Arriving outside the city gate, he prayed for a sign from God—he would choose the woman who when asked for water would offer also to water his camels. The servant wanted a thoughtful, considerate woman for his master's son and prayed to know her by actions rather than by appearance. Before he had even finished praying, God sent a beautiful virgin who perfectly answered the request! Imagine the servant's breathless anticipation as he watched Rebekah run back and forth to water the camels. His faith was strengthened by seeing God act so quickly.

He decided to act quickly as well; he immediately made his intentions known to Rebekah by offering her gold jewelry and a nose ring—the wedding ring of that era. He was further amazed to discover that she was Abraham's relative and immediately bowed and worshipped the Lord. When Rebekah saw this, she must have understood that her desitiny had been determined by God himself and ran to tell her family. Her older brother and protector, Laban, brought the servant home to meet the rest of the clan. After hearing the exciting story of the day's events, they knew their special little girl was chosen by God and agreed for her to go with the servant.

However, the following morning Rebekah's mother and brother were reluctant to let her go so soon. They asked the servant to stay 10 days or so, to delay his mission—God's mission—so they could say good-bye. Rebekah's father, Bethuel, apparently was not part of this plan. While Rebekah chose to leave immediately, she had witnessed something that planted the seed of manipulation in her character. In a time when fathers made all the decisions for the family, Rebekah's mother set a bad example. Rebekah learned that it was acceptable to circumvent her husband's decisions regarding the children and would later do the same thing in her own family.

Her mother also placed an undue burden on this young girl by playing on her sentimentality when it was clear she needed to follow God. As Rebekah looked one last time at the faces of her family, she was surely tempted to feel guilty rather than content with God's will. A mother can have a powerful impact for good or for bad—a fact that Rebekah would later learn.

Two Nations in Your Womb

Isaac was very happy with the wife the Lord gave him. Having just lost his mother, he was comforted by his new wife. Isaac did not just accept her or appreciate her, he loved her. In the age of arranged marriages this was a blessing. However, after 10 years of marriage, Rebekah was unable to conceive. How frustrated she must have felt. Like her once-barren mother-in-law, she probably knew of the promise given first to Abraham and then to Isaac—the promise that Isaac would have many generations of descendants and that his seed would somehow bless all nations.

The feeling of failure and disappointment must have overwhelmed her. Was she really the woman God had chosen for Isaac? If not, would she be discarded so that Isaac could find a woman who could give him sons? Had God made a mistake at the well that day? She must have waited eagerly month after month (120 in all) to see if her cycle would stop, indicating she was on her way to having a baby. She became pregnant only after Isaac prayed to God on her behalf.

According to God's promise and timing, Rebekah conceived. But she was alarmed at the amount of intense movement in her womb. Instead of hearing from the ultrasound technician, she heard from God himself: twins! Not only would these boys become very different types of people, but they would become two different nations, constantly at odds with each other.

Favoritism. A destructive sin—especially in a family. Isaac and Rebekah played favorites. They identified with the son who was most like each of them—Isaac with Esau and Rebekah with Jacob. As is usually the case, this created jealousy and competitiveness between the brothers. Perhaps if they had begged God for unity in their family or for righteousness in treating both boys fairly, they might have avoided the bitterness Esau and Jacob had toward each other.

I'll Do It My Way

The drama comes to its conclusion. Rebekah was overcome by selfish desire to see her favorite son get his father's blessing. Eavesdropping on Isaac's plan to give Esau the blessing, she devised her own elaborate scheme for Jacob to receive it instead. She directed Jacob to lie to his father and to cheat his brother out of his father's blessing. When Esau found out what had happened, he wept and begged his father to bless him also. But the blessing had been given and could not be reclaimed. Isaac's leftover blessing for Esau indicated that although he would serve his younger brother, he would later throw off the yoke.

Rebekah's actions had created in Esau such animosity toward his brother that she was forced to tell Jacob to flee to her family for safety.

Out of his intense anger, one of her children wanted to murder the other. In her grief she tried to save Jacob saying, "Why should I lose both of you in one day?"

Even though God would do great things through Jacob, and his descendants would be as numerous as the stars in the sky, Rebekah's sinful nature ruined the end of her life. In her old age she could have enjoyed the admiration of her husband, children and grandchildren. In the beginning of her marriage Rebekah saw so clearly the hand of God, but in the end she tried to work circumstances out according to her own desires. The last statement made about Rebekah is that she was "disgusted with living" because of Esau's marriages. The beautiful young virgin, full of the promise of the Lord, became a bitter, unhappy old woman.

God's Will and Not My Own

Blind faith is going and doing a task with no knowledge of the outcome. Blind faith is signing the contract and allowing God to fill in the particulars later. God's will always outweighs our will. God's dream to expand the kingdom is always bigger than our dreams.

When Cory and I became Christians in Chicago in November 1990, we had no idea what God had planned for our lives. We were four months old in the Lord when we heard the announcement that the Los Angeles church needed disciples to help build the church. It never crossed our minds to leave our house, great jobs and family; however, God had different plans. Since Cory was a former professional basketball player and I was a model, we received a phone call from a couple we did not know—Kip and Elena McKean—who asked us to consider helping with the Arts/Media/Sports ministry.

We thought to ourselves, "NO WAY." We were just getting our lives back together. Both our house and marriage were being remodeled, and we had excellent jobs. Kip and Elena were kind and simply asked us to pray and to read the book of Esther. The next day Cory and I came to our senses and remembered our Luke 14 commitment to go anywhere and give up everything for Jesus. We packed up and headed to L.A. in two weeks with no jobs and no full-time ministry offer. God honored our blind faith 10 months later with the opportunity to be *Esthers* for him. We were asked to lead the ministry to the Middle East.

Sentimentally, I can relate to Rebekah as she looked into the faces of her family. As I write this, we are preparing to leave for the Middle East tomorrow morning. Americans are advised not to travel there, but we are convinced that the kingdom must advance. Thankfully, God doesn't give us "a spirit of timidity, but a spirit of power, of love and of self-discipline" (2 Timothy 1:7). I trust that God will provide for our saftey. God has comforted me by providing my father, who became a disciple a year ago, to take care of the kids.

"Cast your cares on the Lord and he will sustain you; he will never let the righteous fall" (Psalm 55:22). As Cory and I minister to this part of the world in which Rebekah lived, I choose, like she chose, to go wherever he calls me. I pray to stay faithful to the end—according to his desires and not my own.

Megan Blackwell
Los Angeles, California

 It is easy to become comfortable in our Christian lives. Take a minute to do a heart check. Are you still ready to go anywhere or do anything that you believe is God's will for your life?

6

RACHEL

Genesis 29–35; Ruth 4:11; Matthew 2:18

As God's promises to Abraham continued to be fulfilled, a tense story unfolded. Isaac and his wife Rebekah had twin sons, of whom Isaac favored the older and Rebekah the younger. Esau as the older son was due the blessing—an inheritance not of property or position but of the promises of God. Jacob, the younger son, coveted this blessing which Esau took for granted. Esau's casual regard for his birthright set the stage for Jacob's opportunism and deceit. When Jacob succeeded in supplanting his brother, Esau vowed to murder him as soon as their father was dead.

Rebekah persuaded Isaac to send Jacob away in search of a wife, promoting her favorite son's welfare in two ways. First, this put a safe distance between Jacob and his brother, and second, it ensured that Jacob would not marry one of the heathen Canaanites among whom the family lived.

His very first day in the maternal homeland of Paddan-Aram, Jacob met the beautiful Rachel. For Jacob, it was love at first sight! There were two obstacles to their marriage: the practice of polygamy and the etiquette of marrying one's daughters eldest first. And so the deceiver Jacob became the deceived. Rachel's father Laban gave Jacob his elder daughter Leah, unrecognizable under her heavy bridal veiling. The deception had even more sting because Jacob, having completed seven years of labor to pay for Rachel's hand, was required to pledge seven more to have her.

Polygamy must present significant practical and emotional challenges without the complications of the wives being siblings, one unloved and the other barren.◆

"Give me children, or I'll die!" The poignant plea of a woman torn and gripped by the stigma of an ancient culture. To have a womb that would never bring forth fruit, to have breasts that would never nurse a child, this was a fate worse than death! The mere thought of this led Rachel to desperation. She would do anything. Consumed day and night by her yearning to bear children, she would consider any method. No cost would be too high. She looked for any way to wipe away her disgrace.

Muddled Motives

Few of us have ever felt so driven. With motivation like Rachel's, we could reach many godly goals and fulfill many purposes. Few have ever known such desperation. By rights Jacob could have divorced her for not producing an heir.

The pressure became intense. The motives became muddled. Was her love for Jacob so intense that she could not bear letting him down? Perhaps this stigma destroyed her self-esteem. Did she feel less a woman because of this curse? Or was the obligation to her family the strongest pull?

Initially, Rachel's love for Jacob was very strong. After all, he was the answer to any girl's dreams. At their first meeting, her incredible beauty gave him such a surge of adrenaline that he single-handedly rolled away a huge stone from the mouth of the well—a feat normally requiring the strength of several men (Genesis 29:1-12). No price was too great for her hand in marriage. Even when the dowry of seven years labor became 14, his love did not wane. How could she keep from loving a man whose heart flowed with such total devotion and undying love?

It was obvious that he loved Rachel far more than Leah. Everyone could see it. God could see it, too, and he had compassion on Leah and gave her children. Four sons had been born to Jacob and Leah when Rachel lashed out against her husband with that woeful lament, "Give me children, or I'll die!" What had once been Rachel's desire to fulfill God's purpose for her as a woman and wife turned into a self-focused and self-gratifying desire. She became pregnant with anger, hatred and jealousy. The source of these sins was ingratitude and discontent.

Abundantly Blessed

Rachel's self-pity blinded her to the many things for which she should have been grateful. In a time of arranged marriages, when each spouse was motivated solely by duty, Rachel had a marriage filled with love and devotion. Her husband was not only loving, but godly and hardworking. Having learned from his past, Jacob allowed his character to be molded and became a righteous example for Rachel. He did everything excellently, bringing prosperity to his father-in-law and to himself. His honesty testified for him over and over again. God had truly given Rachel a man she could imitate and follow. But she didn't appreciate that—she wanted children.

As a result of Jacob's hard work, Rachel lived a very secure life. By the time they left Haran to go back to Bethel he was a wealthy man, in spite of the many tricks played on him by Laban. "In this way, the man grew exceedingly prosperous and came to own large flocks, and maidservants and menservants, and camels and donkeys" (Genesis 30:43). But that wasn't enough—Rachel wanted children.

Manipulation and Mandrakes

Her ingratitude and discontent led her to try to circumvent the plan of God. She gave her maidservant, Bilhah, to Jacob as a surrogate. "Here is my maid Bilhah; go in to her, that she may *bear upon my knees* and that I too may have children through her" (Genesis 30:3 NRSV). She was willing to take another woman's child as her own. Although this was an accepted practice in those days, it appears on Rachel's part to be a sort of fantasy. Picture Bilhah actually giving birth into the lap of Rachel, as though Rachel were really giving birth.

Even after the birth of the child, Rachel showed no evidence of gratitude. The name she gave this first son was Dan, meaning *God has vindicated me.* In other words, *God has given me what I really deserve* (Genesis 30:4-6).

A second time Bilhah conceived and bore a son. Rachel named this son Naphtali *(struggle)*, saying "I had a great struggle with my sister, and I have won." Her discontentment led to arrogance and bitterness. The sister with whom she had shared her childhood became her hated rival.

Most astounding is the stark contrast of Leah's attitude. Despite being the unloved partner in this triangle, she gave her children names like Gad *(good fortune)*, Asher *(happy)*, Issachar *(reward)* and Zebulun *(honor)*. The one who had everything to complain about was the most grateful.

Rachel's next desperate move involved the mandrakes that Reuben had found in the field. To get them Rachel was willing to give up a night with her husband. Why did she covet them so? It was because this plant was considered an aphrodisiac and was believed to aid in conception. An ancient fertility drug. There was surely method in Rachel's madness.

Grateful or Greedy?

Even though she was so busy working things out on her own, "God remembered Rachel; he listened to her and opened her womb" (Genesis 30:22). Praise God! Finally the yearned-for, long-awaited son took away her disgrace. How grateful she must have been. "She named him Joseph, and said, 'May the Lord add to me another son'" (Genesis 30:24). Was she grateful or greedy? It seems that her desire was to be "one son up" on Leah.

Rachel's indifference towards God's grace continued to harden her and to lead her into the sins of greed, theft and deceit. Jacob desired to be reconciled to his brother and moved his family and his possessions back to his homeland. Rachel was still discontent with all that God had given her. Knowing that having possession of her father's household gods would ensure an inheritance in her father's estate, she stole them. Had not the God of Jacob done enough for her yet?

"Or I'll Die"

It's hard to comprehend God's love for us. He even gives to the most undeserving, to those most oblivious of his generosity and benevolence. After Jacob and his family left Bethel, Rachel began with great difficulty to give birth to another son. With her dying breath she named him Ben-Oni, meaning *son of my trouble*. But Jacob had the last word. After her death, he changed the child's name to Benjamin, which means *son of my right hand*. Understandably, Jacob was grateful for the sons that his beloved Rachel had borne him. They became the favored sons, the ones Jacob protected and had by his right hand until his death.

Ironically, the one who wanted children or death, died having children. In reality, her discontentment destroyed her long before her physical death. Her life after Joseph's birth was undoubtedly far from fulfilling, She lived only to have another child, then died giving birth to him.

What started as a life of conviction and determination, ended in a desire to be vindicated, to win, to prove herself by bearing children. Rachel was too blind to see Jacob's love or to appreciate God's blessings. She was obsessed with a purpose. On the surface it might have appeared to be the purpose for which God created her a woman, but deep down it was her own self-serving, impotent purpose—to prove her worth apart from God.

Grateful Means Fruitful

"Give me children, or I'll die." This could have been my own cry years ago as I struggled with my inability to conceive. Years past, options were tried, yet nothing happened. I felt the anguish and desperation that Rachel felt. However, over the last few months, as I have come to know

Rachel and have "lived" with her, I recognized a far more disturbing similarity in our characters: ingratitude.

I would not have called myself ungrateful. I appreciate the many blessings God has given me. I have an incredible husband and three wonderful children. Every time I've given something up for God, he has returned to me a hundredfold. I am known for my generosity. But I now see a kind of ingratitude that I have not previously identified. I now understand that true gratitude toward God must *always* be displayed by fulfilling *his* purpose for my life—to personally bear fruit for him, to bring others to know him.

This is not really news to me. I have always believed it and have been fruitful many times. Yet, I see similarities with Rachel when my motives become muddled like hers. Why do I share God's love with others? Is it out of duty? Is it to save face since I know that a "good disciple" has this primary purpose in life? Do I share my faith to win the approval of godly people around me? Do I do it because it is my job?

False motives do not result in a blessing. When my motives are impure, competitiveness and mediocrity set in. I become satisfied with someone else's fruit born "upon my knees." The only pure motive for sharing my faith is the desire to express gratitude to God for my salvation and to bring glory to his name. If I am not bearing fruit as a disciple, I will die (John 15).

Even as I began to study Rachel, I struggled with lack of personal fruit in my life. My prayer now is the same as David's when he recognized his sin. "Create in me a pure heart...restore to me the joy of my salvation and grant me a willing spirit...Then I will teach transgressors your ways" (Psalm 51:10-13).

My heart has changed and the fruit is ripening for the harvest. Out of a pure heart I can now cry out to God, "Give me children, or I'll die." Amen!

Jeannie Fredrick
Abington, Pennsylvania

FOCUS **?** How desperate are you to bear fruit for God? What motivates you to share your faith?

7

POTIPHAR'S WIFE

3

LIKE A ROARING LION

Genesis 37:36, 39:1-23

Joseph was content in Canaan with his family. The son of Jacob (Israel) and his favored wife Rachel, he enjoyed the special attention of his father from whom he received an ornamented coat emphasizing his importance. After sharing two prophetic dreams portraying his family bowing down to him, he found himself the focus of the hate and jealousy of his 11 brothers.

As a 17-year-old he went to visit his brothers who were grazing their father's flocks. In their jealousy, they stripped him of his coat, the symbol of their father's favoritism, and threw him into an empty cistern (a deep hole hewn out of rock in which rainwater was collected and stored). In a final act of cruelty they sold him to Arabian merchants traveling by caravan to Egypt. Dipping his coat into the blood of a young goat, they told their father he was killed by a wild beast.

Upon arriving in Egypt, Joseph was sold to Potiphar, the captain of Pharaoh's guard (chief of the bodyguards and executioners). Egypt was known for many things at this point in history—one being its women who were given to self-indulgence and moral laxity. Potiphar's wife was no exception.◆

A pampered and purposeless woman. A well-built and handsome teenage boy under her authority. Fertile ground for the growth of sin in the heart of a godless woman. Potiphar's wife was an Egyptian. Joseph was a Hebrew slave. Society dictated severe social restrictions; it was considered detestable for an Egyptian even to eat with a Hebrew. But, somehow, sin knows no restrictions.

Estranged from his family and unable to return home to resolve his pain, Joseph served in the house of Potiphar. He had been promoted to a position of authority in the household of this Egyptian official. Because of Joseph's relationship with his God, all of his work was blessed. His master prospered. "The blessing of the Lord was on everything Potiphar had, both in the house and in the field" (Genesis 39:5). Entrusting Joseph with all the household responsibilities, Potiphar concerned himself with nothing but the food he ate (39:6).

A Dangerous Setting

The wife of Potiphar certainly would have had no household responsibilities. Probably most of her pursuits were superficial in nature—decorating the house, seeing to her beauty treatments, deciding special meals she wanted the servants to fix. If she had children, their needs would have been met by the household slaves. She had only one role—to please her husband.

With her private life in order, all that was left was time, and plenty of it, with no outlet to consume her passions. She was idle. She was lonely.

Joseph, a handsome and strong young man, was constantly on the scene when her husband was not. Potiphar was obviously naive or dull to his wife's needs to have created such a dangerous setting. Joseph was not only physically attractive, but his character and spiritual attributes would have made him all the more intriguing.

The day-in and day-out routine of household matters posed a proprietal challenge for both Joseph and the wife of Potiphar in social interactions. Nora Lofts wrote:

> In her presence he was forced, by etiquette and custom, to be as sexless as an attendant eunuch, less assertive than the little dog which lay at the hem of her skirt, for the palace life in the East managed to combine the closest intimacy of service with the most rigid discipline of behavior so that the slave who must, in the course of his duties, be familiar with her very bed chamber, might, at the same time, not even know the colour of her eyes or the form of her headdress.
>
> Such intimacy and such remoteness could become a subtle form of torment *(Women and the Old Testament,* page 46).

The circumstances would have played on the mutual loneliness, needs and attractiveness of both individuals. Although it is not stated that she was attractive, it is likely that the wife of a high official was handpicked and beautiful—an ornament to his life and position.

Sinful Advances

After a time, "his master's wife cast longing eyes on Joseph," and she *suggested* to Joseph, "Come to bed with me" (39:7). Even if Potiphar's wife had some trace of virtue, over time she allowed it to be worn down by her desire for the handsome Hebrew. Whether immediately or over a long period, passion ruled this wealthy Egyptian woman, and she violated three taboos: the Egyptian-Hebrew distinction, the marriage covenant and the master-slave relationship. Had she been caught, the wife of the captain of the guard would have been disgraced.

Joseph refused her advances with a ready response, indicating that he may have foreseen this predicament and prayed God would provide a way out. His multiple reasons for refusal fired out quickly, showing his convictions at many levels: his position over the master's household, his loyalty to Potiphar himself, his reverence for marriage, and his relationship with God.

Potiphar's wife was relentless in her pursuit. One day the house was conveniently vacated. Only the two of them were there. Either she was astute to recognize the opportunity or she set it up. The scenario allowed a bold advance on Joseph. Like a lioness stalking her prey, she approached Joseph. Grabbing his cloak, this time she *demanded,* "Come to bed with me!" (39:12). The godly prey, desperate to escape, fled for his life and his purity, leaving his cloak in her hand. No talk. No excuses. No hesitation.

Joseph made a life-changing decision when he "left his cloak in her hand." His symbol of identity and status was now gone. He was left wide open to false charges and an uncertain future.

Potiphar's wife was in a precarious situation herself. Here was a half-naked, young Hebrew slave running from the house. In her hands was the evidence that could incriminate them both. In many ways she had been discovered. The wife of the guard to the Pharaoh had to act quickly. Out of resentment and humiliation, she devised a scheme to save face.

The Cover-Up

In mock indignation she said to her household servants, "Look, this Hebrew has been brought to us to make sport of us! He came in here to sleep with me, but I screamed. When he heard me scream for help, he left his cloak beside me and ran out of the house" (39:14-15). Potiphar's wife acted shrewdly as she built her case with the incriminating evidence "beside her."

By the time Potiphar came home, his wife had already created an account that not only put the blame on Joseph, but on her husband as well. "That Hebrew slave you brought us came to me to make sport of me. But as soon as I screamed for help, he left his cloak beside me and ran out of the house (39:17-18)."

Potiphar "burned with anger," and took Joseph and put him in prison. Nothing more is said of this woman. Joseph initially paid the price for her lust, her pride and her deceit. But unless she subsequently repented, she paid the ultimate price.

One wonders what the wife of the bodyguard to the Pharaoh was thinking when Joseph was later vindicated and placed over all of Egypt, including the captain of the guard and his whole household. Surely "the Lord detests [a woman] of perverse heart, but he delights in those whose ways are blameless" (Proverbs 11:20).

Let Go of Pride

"Be self-controlled and alert. Your enemy the devil prowls around like a roaring lion looking for someone to devour" (1 Peter 5:8).

Bold and brazen, Potiphar's wife was anything but subtle in her pursuit of Joseph. Like the hungry lion, she stalked her prey and waited patiently for just the right moment to attack. In the same way, Satan's eyes are always on me. I'm never out of range for an attack. He is relentless in his quest, always deceitful, showing no mercy. He patiently waits for just the right opportunity to strike.

For years I was not aware of the web of pride subtly woven throughout my heart. I never had realized its destructive effects or understood its consequences. Honestly, I had never really seen myself as prideful, just as someone with opinions—strong opinions. When I wasn't voicing my opinions, I was stuffing them, becoming critical and resentful.

My marriage was falling apart and my relationships with my children (especially my daughter) were suffering as a result of my pride. It took some dear friends like Ron and Linda Brumley, Bruce and Robyn Williams, and my husband, John, to confront me. But because of my stubborn heart, I was unable to see my sin for months. I used excuses like ignorance and past hurts to keep me from feeling the pain and accepting the responsibility.

I spent hours searching the Scriptures to prove my position, only to end up being convicted of my sin. "God opposes the proud," "Pride comes before the fall," and "Wisdom hates pride and arrogance" were passages that kept running through my mind.

I needed to accept that my pride was sin. I'll never forget Robyn's words, "Just let go, Nancy." In my stubbornness, I didn't think I could *let go.* I didn't understand what I was to let go *of.*

Satan had a tight hold on me. But, thankfully, God had a stronger hold. I needed to trust that God was sovereign, that he who judges justly would be the one to judge my life.

Finally, everything clicked. If I were to let go of my pride, Satan would have to let go of his hold on my life. Then I would be free! I did and I am. My attitude toward my *enemy* became like David's toward his:

> I pursued my enemies and overtook them; I did not turn back
> till they were destroyed. I crushed them so that they could not
> rise; they fell beneath my feet (Psalm 18:37-38).

Just as Potiphar's wife was not successful in her seductive attack on Joseph, so Satan will no longer be successful in *pride* attacks on me. Now that I see the pride that was once hidden, I will flee. No talk. No excuses. No hesitation.

Nancy Mannel
Chicago, Illinois

 How aware are you that Satan, the hungry lion, is stalking you daily? How do you guard against his attacks?

8

MIRIAM

RESPONSE TO ABILITY

Exodus 2:1-10, 15:19-21; Numbers 12; Micah 6:3-4

Building pyramids. Suffering mistreatment. Such was the lot of the Israelites in Egypt. The family of Joseph originally moved to Egypt to escape the famine in their native land. Because of his appreciation and respect for Joseph, the Pharaoh treated his family graciously. But 430 years later, there was no soft spot in the heart of the reigning Pharaoh for these strong and numerous descendants of Joseph. Fear of their possible alliance with Egypt's enemies had driven the authorities to enslave and, thus, control the people.

God heard the cries of his people and worked his plan to honor his promise to Abraham, Joseph's great-grandfather. He prepared and sent Moses and Aaron to lead his people back to the land of Canaan—the land originally promised to Abraham and his descendants. From this family of leaders emerged not only Moses and Aaron, but a leader among women—their older sister, Miriam. ◆

S he was probably no more than 10 years old when the Bible first introduces her in Exodus. But she was fast-thinking. Articulate. Bold. Responsible. Miriam stood watch over her three-month-old brother—one of the doomed baby boys of the Israelite slaves. After one last nursing from her full breasts, Moses' mother had placed him lovingly in a waterproof basket—to float among the reeds along the bank of the Nile River. In a last desperate attempt to save his life she had set him afloat with a prayer to the one God of the Hebrew nation. God's plan unfolded as he placed his hand firmly on this little one who would someday lead his mother, sister and all of Israel out of Pharaoh's cruel clutches. Redemption in a basket.

A Moment of Destiny

As Miriam watched—holding her breath, her heart beating wildly—Pharaoh's daughter and her entourage came to the river to bathe. Seeing the basket and probably hearing the piercing cries of the baby, she called for her servant girl to bring the basket to her. As soon as she opened it, her heart was touched—a royal and pampered heart, but a heart of compassion nonetheless. God answered the prayer of a desperate Hebrew woman who loved her child. This same God placed Miriam at a pivotal point in history. He chose for this young girl to play a crucial role in the deliverance of his people.

Miriam did not hesitate, but seized the moment. The child of a slave ran up unannounced to the daughter of a king and asked clearly, confidently and shrewdly, "Shall I go and get one of the Hebrew women to nurse the baby for you?" The question was certainly a sensible one— they both knew that many Hebrew women were experiencing heavy hearts as well as heavy breasts. Miriam's ability to react quickly, to think through the twist of offering to get a woman to nurse the baby (her own mother) shows mental agility and finesse that were beyond her years. God had given leadership qualities to this young slave girl—qualities he would mold and use to give direction to his people.

All the Women Followed Her

Eighty years later soul-piercing cries and moans came from every house in Egypt. The final plague was delivered—death of the firstborn. The pain and fear were intense. Finally, a prideful ruler was brought to his knees—though only briefly. Pharaoh let the people go. The Bible says in Exodus 14:8 that they marched out *boldly*. Two verses later, we are told that they were *terrified*. Pharaoh decided he did not want to lose his slave labor after all. Sandwiched between the Red Sea and the world's most powerful army, the Israelites gave up. They became faithless. But Moses did what God called him to do. In faith he led the people. In love God delivered the people.

On the safe side of the sea Miriam, the prophetess, took a tambourine in her hand and sang. "All the women followed her, with tambourines and dancing" (Exodus 15:20). The little 10-year-old, quick-thinking, responsible girl had grown up to become a prophetess—a special woman of God. His hand guided her as surely it did her brothers, Moses and Aaron, the prophets, the leaders of God's exodus.

She led the women in praising God, in giving thanks for the love and protection he had given his oppressed people. She was a woman of influence. God had raised her up to be a leader among her peers. He needed her to be the role model for over 600,000 displaced women. They had left everything that was familiar to them. Being slaves was certainly not a life of choice, but they did have their own homes and their own schedules. They basically knew what to expect in their day-to-day routines. At this point, everything was upside down, and God gave them security and stability through their leader, Miriam. So along with the talent he gave her great responsibility—responsibility bringing a deep need to stay close to her God. A strong leader can begin to lead for herself and for her own glory if she does not stay close to her God. This is a lesson Miriam was soon to learn.

Unchecked Pride

Several months into the journey, we get a glimpse into the temptation that Miriam experienced. We also see the sin born out of that temptation.

"We are special messengers of God too," reasoned Aaron and Miriam as they fed on each other's jealousy. In an attempt to discredit Moses and to "credit" themselves, they made an issue of his marriage to Zipporah, a Cushite woman.

It is no coincidence that the Spirit reminds us that "Moses was a humble man, more humble than anyone else on the face of the earth" (Numbers 12:3). The darkness of their arrogance caused the light of his humility to shine more brightly. Moses as God's specially chosen leader was not possessive of power, protective of position, or threatened by inclusion.

In Numbers 11 God had taken of the Spirit that was on Moses and had filled the 70 elders, causing them to prophesy. Two other leaders began to prophesy back in the camp. Joshua, Moses' loyal aid, was horrified. "Stop them," he cried to Moses.

"Are you jealous for my sake? I wish that all the Lord's people were prophets and that the Lord would put his Spirit on them" (11:29). He did not feel a need to hold on to his authority. He was a humble man, a man who knew that God gives authority and recalls authority. He knew that God was in control, so he was secure in his leadership.

It was against a humble man like this that Miriam spoke. A man who had never wanted to speak or lead or be in the spotlight. A man who only led in obedience to God. Instead of being convicted by his righteous leadership, Miriam, in the weakness of her sinful nature, focused on a perceived weakness in his life. Blowing it out of proportion, she enlarged it to eclipse his godly life. Then she self-righteously revelled in her role and her importance. In her arrogance and criticalness, she attacked the integrity of a man who knew the God of the universe face-to-face. Audacity. Raw arrogant audacity. And she could not even see it.

I could do it better, or at least as well, she thought. *Why don't I get more attention? More credit?* Her arrogance was her shame—and God showed her very clearly both who was in control and how destructive her sin was. When the cloud of discipline lifted, she stood before her brothers white with leprosy. As the disease ate away her skin, her sin ate away her joy, her security, her purpose. God made the point that this was a serious matter. Her disdain and disrespect for God was destructive—to her and to others.

God, in love and protection for his people, had to make an example of Miriam. Because she was a high-profile spiritual leader, both women and men would have been affected by her arrogant second-guessing of Moses and of God. In order to lead a million-plus people through a desert, Moses needed the loyal support of his fellow leaders. Miriam had taken her eyes off her mission and had put them on herself.

Moses in his humility was not threatened by her divisive talk, her critical murmuring. He did not jump to the defense of himself or his wife. He knew who was in control. He loved God and he loved his sister. His concern was not his position; it was his sister, and he begged God to heal her.

God did graciously restore Miriam's health, but he first humbled her by confining her outside the camp for seven days. God made sure everyone knew what had happened through inflicting the leprosy and through detaining a nation for her to learn her lesson. *"The people did not move"* while one of their leaders was reminded that God is God and is unquestionably worthy of our respect. Miriam had begun to lead for herself and for her glory and had not stayed close to her God.

Possibly the reason Miriam was disciplined so strongly by God is because she was the instigator. Aaron had a weak, easily influenced character, evidenced by his giving in to the people's idolatry and by his blame-shifting (Exodus 32). Miriam was the strong one. She was the one who could think quickly, who could manipulate situations to achieve her desired selfish goal.

It's my guess that Miriam was forever changed by her leprous encounter with God. Being called before him and disciplined directly by his hand is something she would never have forgotten. Seeing her once healthy skin rotting and falling off in pieces in less than 60 seconds would have made a lasting impact. God longed to bless humility in her heart. I am sure that whenever she was again tempted to second-guess God or to be critical of Moses or other leaders, she remembered. Moses did not want the people to forget either: "Remember what the Lord your God did to Miriam along the way after you came out of Egypt" (Deuteronomy

24:9). Even in her sin, Miriam was used by God to teach his people to be humble and not to oppose the One who loved them.

A God of Grace

Over five centuries later God spoke through his prophet Micah reminding the people of his care for them:

> My people, what have I done to you?
> How have I burdened you? Answer me.
> I brought you up out of Egypt
> and redeemed you from the land of slavery.
> I sent Moses to lead you,
> also Aaron and Miriam (Micah 6:3-4).

God works with his people; he disciplines them, and he uses them in their imperfection. After Miriam's rebellious and arrogant display, hundreds of years later God describes her leadership as a blessing to the people, not a burden. The specific temptation and ensuing sin recorded in Numbers 12 were not the whole of the life of this prophetess. If her leadership was indeed a blessing to the people, then her life must have been characterized by humility, by faith and by perseverance. God gave her talent. Then he molded and disciplined her so she would continue to trust in him and not in her own ability. We can be thankful that God will use our talents for his purposes and that he will purify us in the process—if we keep an open and humble heart before him and others.

Humble Not Critical

Criticalness. Arrogance. Unspiritual thinking. A triad of attitudes that clamor to live in me. When I am not walking closely and humbly with my God, I hear the same whispers in my head that Miriam heard. I want to be in control, to call the shots. Second-guessing smugness slithers into my heart, and I magnify the weaknesses of godly leaders in my life. My perspective seems sharp, clear, insightful. But it is a deception—like when people hallucinating on drugs believe they are receiving a pristine glimpse of reality. When my inner eyes are out of focus, I see what I want to see. I see what everybody else is doing wrong—especially leaders because they are more visible. But when through humility and vulnerability my inner eyes receive corrective lenses, I see what God wants me to see. I see spiritual people who have been given a challenging responsibility—people who are not perfect, but who need my loyal support and encouragement to do what God has called them to do.

When my heart is soft before God and others, I am thankful for the leaders God has placed in my life. I long to make their work a joy, not a burden. Just as Miriam influenced Aaron, so I can influence others negatively by not supporting or affirming—this is just as damaging to the unity of the body as outright divisiveness. Neither helps us move forward as one body, seeking to do the will of our Father together. God does not take this lack of loyalty and submission any more lightly than he did in the desert thousands of years ago.

Although I have never been given a leprous rebuke by God, I have seen how destructive my sin can be. I have learned that when I get critical, I need to get humble. I want to keep a pure heart before God and before both those who lead me and those whom I lead. Only then is my spirit guarded from criticalness, arrogance and unspiritual thinking.

Thank you, God, for corrective lenses. Thank you for forgiveness and the power to change. Thank you for teaching me, as you taught my sister, Miriam, how to be a blessing in the lives of others.

Sheila Jones
Concord, Massachusetts

FOCUS

Who are the examples of humility God has put in your life? Are you learning from them, or are you being critical and trying to find a weakness in them in order to exalt yourself?

9

RAHAB

Joshua 2:1-24, 6:15-25; Matthew 1:5; Hebrews 11:31

God had promised that the world would sit up and take notice when he brought his chosen people out of Egypt. Israel was God's visual aid to people for all time to illustrate a covenant relationship with an all-powerful God. And the world watched. Without satellites, or TV, or radio, or even newspapers...they watched, and the word spread.

They watched as the reigning world power, Egypt (to whom most of them were subject), was devastated by the 10 plagues. They watched as a ragtag group of slaves stumbled out of Egypt, complaining and camping out in disarray. They watched the fireworks on Mt. Sinai. Spies from other nations peered down on the camp of Israel, and word spread as those former slaves followed orders from their God and were transformed from sloppy disorder to power and dignity.

A majestic tabernacle came to dominate the camp. The tents were pitched in rows by tribe facing the bright blue holy tent. Banners waved; trumpets sounded; marching orders were obeyed. Nation after nation whose armies dared to oppose Israel's passage were defeated, and the word spread.

Though the march from Egypt to the borders of Canaan took only six months, Israel had wandered in the desert for an additional 40 years as a result of her faithlessness. Yet, God had not deserted her, giving military victories that made both Israel and her God legendary. Crossing the Jordan, Israel's army entered the rich land of Canaan. God's battle plan was audacious—the Israelites were to assault the mighty fortified walls of Jericho. Within that city lived a woman named Rahab.♦

She was a harlot. Her house was part of the wall surrounding the city of Jericho. Even then, 2,000 years ago, God was determining the time and place for Rahab to live so that she could have the opportunity to reach out and find him. How often she must have sat by her window and looked out at the road leading to the Jordan River. Perhaps she would watch the travelers with their loads as they approached the city gates. Perhaps she would look up at the hills and wonder about her own life—her significance, her family, her future.

The God of the Israelites

We do not know when or why she turned to prostitution—the oldest
of professions—sex for pay. She was a pagan. The city where she lived
did not know the God of the Israelites. Yet Rahab had heard about this
God. She had heard the stories of this lucky nation (chosen people)
whose God had parted the Red Sea. Everyone in Jericho had heard how
God had destroyed Og and Sihon, the kings of the Amorites, because of
their disobedience. This God gave victories to his people.

How did these stories affect the people of Jericho? The Bible says,
"The hearts of the people melted and became as water" (Joshua 7:5).
Maybe the women talked about it in fear as they washed their clothes and
ground their grain. Perhaps the men scoffed but inwardly feared for
their lives and the lives of their families. Did the travelers spread the
stories? Did the men who frequented Rahab's place talk about it among
themselves and to her as well? I wonder how Rahab felt when she heard
these fearsome stories.

Rahab, amid the talk, continued with the routine of her life. She
expected nothing unusual. Then, one day at dusk, two foreigners
knocked at her door. Why had they come? Were they customers coming
for services so early in the evening? Rahab was accustomed to letting
strange men into her house. However, these men had not come to her
for the reason she had thought. These two young Israelites were sent
by God to spy out Jericho for future capture.

A Decision of Faith

Now she was trapped. She had to make an important decision. Surely
people would know these men were here. What should she do? Perhaps
the men asked her to hide them. Perhaps she volunteered. Whichever,
we do know that their presence presented her with a choice—a window
of opportunity. They offered her the honor of being useful to their God.
That is what the word *holy* means—"set apart for God's use." Isn't that
just like our God! He chooses the unlikely (the unchosen), does the
unexpected, calls things that are not as though they were. Here, he calls
a harlot to be holy.

Rahab recognized the opportunity when it came. She seized the
opportunity. But why? And how did she know this was from God?

Somehow, some way, God had planted in her the seed of faith. And
now, in fear, her faith came to fruition. "By faith...she welcomed the
spies" (Hebrews 11:31). Rahab had faith! She believed what she had

heard about this God who cared for his people. God sent these two men into her world—placing her in jeopardy with the authorities and with the status quo. How did she respond? She "welcomed them"!

One cannot welcome another and at the same time be resistant, begrudging, withholding or condescending. If she had reservations about hiding the spies, she would have obeyed when the king ordered her to "bring out the men who came to you" (Joshua 2:3).

Rahab could have exposed the spies. She could have said, "They are hiding on my rooftop underneath the flax. Go and get them." However, she was no longer living by her feelings. She had begun a new journey of faith. That faith compelled her to protect the spies. She did not back down out of cowardice or spite. No doubt it was Rahab's nature to be crafty and deceitful. (The Bible uses those terms to define the nature of the prostitute in Proverbs 7:10.) In fact, she lied about where the spies were. Yet, God saw in her heart something that pleased him. When the window of opportunity opened, she made a decision based on faith—Rahab was becoming a woman of faith.

A Godly Bargain

In faith, Rahab sent the pursuers away and went to the roof to plea-bargain with the Israelite spies. She had a goal in mind. Realizing Jericho's fate, she wanted to save her family. Even though she was a sinful woman, she cared about her father and mother and brothers and sisters. She had been living in fear since she had heard those stories of Sihon and Og. She feared for her father and brothers when she heard "their sons were slain" (Numbers 21:29). She feared for herself and her sisters when she heard "their daughters were taken captive." When she had heard of "complete destruction" (Numbers 21:30), she had been so frightened! Yet now, her newfound faith had routed her fears, and boldly she bargained with these men.

Her petition was specific—she wanted God to save her family from death, and she wanted a sign. The spies responded, "Our lives for yours." Yes! That was the response she had hoped for! Because of her faith, her family could be saved. Rahab gave the spies information about the land; then she let them down by a rope out her window. Before they left, they tossed up to her the scarlet cord—the sign.

She listened to their instructions: "When we capture Jericho, this scarlet cord must be tied in the same window through which you let us escape" (Joshua 2:18).

"Agreed," she replied. What did she think as she clutched the cord in her fingers? Why not a brown cord like the rope? Why scarlet? Why the color of blood? Why the escape window? Was God going to tie her in to his own people through her own Passover experience? She probably knew nothing of the blood on the doorposts that had saved the Israelite firstborn from death years earlier. But she did know she believed these men were coming back. She firmly tied the cord in the window. There it was visible to all. Yet, among her people, it held meaning only for her. It was her sign—her God-sent visual aid. If her faith grew weak in the coming days, she could look at the cord. She could remember. It did happen. I made a decision. I helped those men. They will be back.

Faith Rewarded

Rahab persevered in her faith as the days passed. God was preparing his people for the conquest. They were busy crossing the Jordan River and camping at Gilgal. What was Rahab doing during this time? We do not know, but she kept that cord in her window. You see, she did not lose her faith.

By this time, Jericho was tightly shut up because of the Israelites. As Rahab looked out her window, she no longer saw a stream of travelers. It was a tense time in a city of fear. What did they talk about now as they washed their clothes and ground their grain?

Unlike the others, Rahab must have spoken in private with hope, not with fear. She must have told her parents about the special agreement, about the scarlet cord. Because she loved them, she shared her faith with her family. She was a persuasive woman. She persuaded them to be part of the plan.

Then came the day she had longed for. She looked out her window for the last time. She saw God's people marching around her city. She heard the trumpets and the shouts. And the walls of the city came tumbling down. The destruction was complete—except for Rahab and her family. God was faithful. It is his nature. What brought destruction to the disobedient (unfaithful) brought salvation to the faithful. (The smell of death to one is the aroma of life to another—2 Corinthians 2:15-16.) Faith made the difference. You see, she and her family were saved by faith.

Rahab's decision of faith forever changed her life. It changed the lives of her family. More than that, she made a difference for all of God's people.

What became of her? She was a transformed woman. God filled her life with newness. Everything was new. She lived among the Israelites. She married an Israelite. She gave birth to a son of her own. She named him Boaz. He's the one who married Ruth. From them came Jesse and King David and the "root of Jesse"—Jesus. From this woman, this harlot, this sinner—a Savior was born. You see, a harlot can be holy by faith.

My Scarlet Cords

I am inspired by Rahab. When I lived in Bangkok, Thailand, I often thought of her. That pagan city is known for its prostitution. I wondered how many potential *Rahabs* were living there. I longed to see them come to have faith, to see God's window of opportunity in their lives. A society with no standard leaves its people numbed in heart. That is where Rahab was in her heart until she heard about a God who cared for his people.

First, I learned from Rahab the solution to numbness of heart. When my heart is not moved by the lost or by my own sins, I need what she needed. I need to remember God's love. If I let my heart become numb, I will not recognize the opportunities God is arranging in my life. Whenever I see I am not welcoming the people and situations God sends to me, my heart is numb, and I am not living by faith.

Rahab listened to those stories, and her heart was softened, and her faith grew. She did not have a Bible to read. I do. And so do you. She must have looked at that scarlet cord every day just to help her remember.

What are the *scarlet cords* God has given me?

1. The Bible. I can see in black and white that he loves me, that he has expectations and a plan for me.

2. My heritage. God gave me parents who honored God and lived by his word. I remember their lives and how God used them to plant the seeds of faith in my heart.

3. My baptism. This act of faith is a major scarlet cord! God graciously gave me a time and place so that I could remember—20 years ago I made the decision to make Jesus Lord. Like Rahab, I acknowledged in my

heart that "the Lord your God is God in heaven above and on the earth below" (Joshua 2:11).

4. The cross. My baptism makes the scarlet cord of the cross meaningful in my life—a tangible sign of God's commitment to me.

5. My marriage. I look at the band on my finger and remember the time and place: June 19, 1982. That was the joyful day God gave me the husband whom I did not deserve. That is when I vowed before God to be faithful and to love my husband always. Remembering that vow has helped me through the difficult times in our marriage when I was tempted to lose faith or to withhold my love and affection. Looking at this cord now brings me a greater joy than it did in the beginning.

6. My three children. I look at them, and I remember they are God's blessing. They will imitate my faith or my lack of faith. That makes me want to be faithful.

7. My spiritual children. When I see the lives of those I have helped enter the kingdom, I am reminded that I can and must be useful to him.

I believe that God gives all of us windows of opportunity. If we ask, he will supply a scarlet cord in every window. We must be careful not to close our hearts and shut the window of God's grace, and we must not loose the scarlet cords.

Emily Bringardner
La Crescenta, California

 FOCUS What *scarlet cord* has God put in your life to help you remember his grace to you?

10

DEBORAH

RISING IN STRENGTH

Judges 4:1-5:31

The people who witnessed the conquest under Joshua remained faithful to God. But for whatever reason, they did not instill that faithfulness in the hearts of their children. Judges 2:10 gives us the sad report that "after that whole generation had been gathered to their fathers, another generation grew up, who knew neither the Lord nor what he had done for Israel" (Judges 2:6-23). The people fell headlong into idol worship, prostituting themselves with Baal and Ashtaroth and breaking the heart of their faithful God.

Each time God allowed their rebellion to sell them into slavery to surrounding nations, they cried out for deliverance—bowing once again to the one true God who could save them. Each time his own gracious nature prompted him to raise up a leader who would deliver his people from the clutches of their enemies. As long as this leader, or judge, was alive, God continued to bring victory to the people. After the death of each judge, the people would slide back into the mire of idolatry.

The God-given structure of Israel's loose government called for a male leader. For the most part women played important, but back-seat, roles in the affairs of the nation. But on one especially rare occasion, God did the extraordinary. He did the unpredictable. He raised up a woman to lead his people. She was made to shine as a ray of hope in a time of dark despair. Her name was Deborah.◆

We first meet Deborah sitting under the Palm of Deborah judging disputes among her people. Contrasted with the other judges who were mainly military leaders, she stood as the solitary woman judge. Besides this, she was also a prophetess—a spokesperson for God himself. Just how this woman ascended to the lofty position of being a judge and a prophetess in Israel, we are not told. Just why God would break his own order of things to exalt a women to not only a high position, but a position held only by men both before and after her, we are not told. Surely this was a woman among women—a standout in every sense of the word.

What we do know about this remarkable leader is that she was the wife of an otherwise unknown man, Lappidoth, and that she lived in the hill country of Ephraim. And we know that she was characterized by great faithfulness before God at a time when most of her countrymen were overwhelmed with great fearfulness! Her personal qualities make a long list. She was bold enough to summon the top male military commander and to challenge him to lead the Israelite army into battle with Canaan. And she expected him to do what she asked, for she had the confidence that she was giving the very orders of God. She was humble enough to let Barak, her fearful counterpart, do the actual leading of the army in spite of his cowardice. She was brave enough to personally lure Sisera, the opposing army commander, into battle and then to go into the battle herself (unprecedented for a woman of that day)!

Walking by Faith, Not by Sight

Perhaps her most outstanding quality, however, was the unquestioning faith she had in God at a time when there was little evidence that God was really with the nation. In fact, for 20 years he had not delivered them from the hands of their enemies. Can you imagine what 20 years of oppression would do to the faith of ordinary people? Most of us can muster some faith when there is at least some evidence of God working in our lives. We can take a good situation and develop the faith to make it better. But the ability to look at defeat after defeat while maintaining faith is a staggering proposition indeed. This woman Deborah looked at the circumstances of repeated defeat and expected victory anyway. Amazing! She trusted the words of God, and not her own evaluation of the physical situation. Nor was she influenced negatively by the faithlessness of everyone around her, including even Barak. She didn't simply face the facts—she *faithed* the facts!

When Barak followed the instructions of Deborah and gathered an army, Sisera responded by gathering his army, which included 900 iron chariots. This woman of faith was not shaken in the least, but loaned her faith to Barak with these final challenging words: "Go! This is the day the LORD has given Sisera into your hands. Has not the LORD gone ahead of you?" (Judges 4:14). When great faith exists in people, coupled with obedience, God gives a great victory.

The description of this victory is recorded in Judges 4:15-16 with heart-stirring words:

At Barak's advance, the LORD routed Sisera and all his chariots and army by the sword, and Sisera abandoned his chariot and fled on foot. But Barak pursued the chariots and army as far as Harosheth Haggoyim. All the troops of Sisera fell by the sword; not a man was left.

Hitting the Nail on the Head!

From a woman's perspective, the most exciting part of the battle was yet to come! The sole survivor of the battle mentioned above was the commander Sisera. He fled on foot to the tent of Jael, the wife of Heber the Kennite, who in the past had been on friendly terms with Sisera's king. Whether Heber may have been favorable toward Sisera or not, we do not know. What we do know is that Deborah's example had evidently inspired a nation of women to step outside their household duties and put their hands to the battle. At least that was the case with this women, Jael. She boldly greeted Sisera and cleverly fed him warm milk, which acted as a sedative to this war-weary commander. When he fell into a deep sleep, Jael took a nail, deftly hit the nail on (and into) the head, and the rest is history.

As Deborah had said, the honor for the victory did indeed go to a woman. Barak saw the fulfillment with his own eyes when he came to the tent of this new national heroine and was shown the dead commander. Barak was the third person on the scale of heroes that day, and the two before him were both women!

After the victory, the humility of Deborah was seen in the way that she shared the victory with Barak. As a woman leader of great influence, she was strong but supportive of the male leader in the nation. She was in no way insecure or competitive with him. Whether she was in front leading or in the rear encouraging, she was secure in who she was and in what she was trying to accomplish for her God. Seeking success for God is a very different thing than seeking success for one's self. The beautiful song of victory in Judges 5 was not a solo by Deborah, but a duet with Barak, with whom she shared the celebration. The focus of Deborah's heart was in glorifying God rather than seeking recognition for herself or for Barak. Her marvelous love for God and for her people is expressed wonderfully in these well-known words which began the song (5:2): "When the princes in Israel take the lead, when the people willingly offer themselves—praise the Lord!"

Faithful Not Fearful!

Mistrustful. Afraid of rejection. Afraid to tell anyone who I really was inside. Afraid to let the emotional wall down. Most of my life I was controlled by the sins which I had allowed Satan to sow deep in my heart. Like the Israelites in the days of Deborah, I also felt oppressed. But thank God that I listened to his word and obeyed it in order to be liberated from these crippling sins. Praise God that I had women like Deborah in my life who loved God and me enough to get into my life and help me overcome.

The causes of my mistrust began with having an alcoholic father whose frequent violent actions and rejection set fear into my heart. Through the years I became even more mistrustful of even religious people, especially leaders, because of some bad experiences in the denominational world. To top it off, my husband, a preacher in one of these denominational groups, was often harsh and insensitive toward my feelings. (Thankfully, he became a disciple and has changed dramatically.) Finally, once I became a true disciple, God began to lead me to victory over fear and mistrust. Praise God!

It takes a daily commitment to stay victorious over fearfulness and related sins. Like Deborah, I have to keep listening to God daily. I am a woman chosen by God to speak his words to others. Satan attacks my heart daily in order to stir my fears back into flame, attempting to stop me from carrying out the plans that God has for my life. When I listen to the great promises of the Lord, my faith always overpowers my tendency to fear. As in Judges 5, when Deborah recited the tremendous victories which God had given the Israelites, I must recite the victories which God has given to me and to those other faithful warriors around me.

On a very practical basis, when the fear demon really goes after me, I have to expose the temptations very blatantly. I list out all of the fear temptations on a sheet of paper and cry out to God to rebuke the demon of fear in the name of Jesus. One by one, I surrender each fear temptation to him completely, after which I tear up the paper. Then I write out appropriate promises from God's word which I hold on to as a weapon against Satan for the rest of the day. I thank God in advance for the victory which I then claim by faith. It is very important to go out quickly and do the very thing that has been producing the fear in me. This particular approach, as simple as it is, has also helped many other women deal with all sorts of fears.

As Deborah was filled with gratitude for the victory given by God, I can never thank God enough for the numerous victories he has given me. At age 50, I look back at the past decade and marvel at the wonderful marriage I now have with my precious partner in the gospel, the two grown children who love God as disciples, and the opportunity to live out the answer to the last prayer that Deborah prayed to God: "May they who love you be like the sun when it rises in its strength" (Judges 5:31).

Theresa Ferguson
Danvers, Massachusetts

 How big of a factor are fears in your thinking on a daily basis? How much do they influence your actions? After finishing this article, will you write out a specific plan to conquer them?

11

DELILAH

A CONSTANT DRIPPING

Judges 14-16

A strong man with long hair and a quick temper, Samson was the 13th judge of Israel. His birth was announced by the angel of the Lord to the barren wife of Manoah, a Benjamite. The instructions to the mother-to-be were clear: You are to take a Nazirite vow yourself and you are to ensure that the child will be a Nazirite of God from birth (Numbers 6:1-21). The vow called for no eating or drinking of anything from the grapevine. Also, no razor was to be used on his head.

God set Samson apart as a leader of the Israelites and as a thorn in the side of the Philistines. These people dominated the Israelites and threatened to destroy the lineage of the Hebrews, more through intermarriage and culture absorption than military force. Although Samson was a special instrument used by God to maintain the bloodline of Abraham's promise, he was a man who reflected the spirit of his time—a time in Israel when "every man did what was right in his own eyes" (RSV) (Judges 17:6). What was *right* was what he *wanted*. After a brief, tragic marriage and a tryst with a prostitute, he set his affections on Delilah, a daughter of the Philistines. ◆

Delilah, the woman who betrayed and ruined the spiritual leader of her time. What a way to be remembered! As women, we are to be companions to help the men in our lives. We are not sure what motivated Delilah to deliberately destroy Samson, the man in her life. Her legacy could have been powerful and inspiring had she known or cared enough to follow Samson's God.

She was a beautiful Philistine woman—influential and smart. But she worshipped idols. Her character and her morals reflected her lack of devotion to the true and living God, yet she attracted Samson, the most powerful man of the day.

A Devilish Opportunity

The Philistine leaders saw this relationship as the perfect opportunity to take revenge. After all, Samson was a bitter enemy who had overtaken their army. These leaders offered Delilah immense wealth is she would merely betray Samson—the man who loved her passionately. The greed for money struck, and she immediately agreed to the conspiracy.

Think of it—the leaders, probably five in all, came to her personally, deperately in need of her help. It must have made her feel very important. Her role suddenly changed from being a mistress to being a key figure in a national conspiracy. The leaders desperately needed her. She would become a woman of power, influence and wealth. To Delilah, this was an incredible opportunity for easy success.

Honestly, we do not know what motivated Delilah to act. It could have been the money, personal pride, a misplaced desire to help her people or even the opportunity to humiliate a powerful, godly man like Samson. Whatever the reason, she immediately acted decisively with no seeming regret or sentimentality.

Learning the Secret

The plan was for Delilah to learn the secret of Samson's strength. How could he could be tied up and subdued? The Philistine rulers told Delilah to "lure" (i.e. *seduce*) Samson into sharing this secret. Three times Delilah demanded the answer, and three times Samson replied falsely. After each incident Delilah became more and more angry.

Frustrated by not getting her way, Delilah resorted to accusing Samson of not loving her—the ultimate emotional weapon. "'How can you say "I love you," when you won't confide in me? This is the third time you have made a fool of me and haven't told me the secret of your great strength.' With such nagging, she prodded him day after day until he was tired to death" (Judges 16:15-16). She became that annoying, constant dripping described in Proverbs 27:15.

She cajoled him into being open with her in order to attack him in his vulnerability. Finally, Samson gave in and told her the truth: "If my head were shaved, my strength would leave me, and I would become as weak as any other man" (Judges 16:17).

The secret was out. The stage was set. It was the ultimate defeat. Feigning gentleness, she cradled his head in her lap and destroyed the man who had trusted her. She called for a fellow conspirator to shave off the seven braids of his hair, rendering him powerless.

After his capture, the Philistines humiliated him by gouging out his eyes and set him to grinding out the grain in the prison. The Spirit of the Lord had left Samson. What a horrible end for a mighty warrior. He had foolishly sold his birthright for the affections of an unfaithful woman.

One Last Hurrah!

In honor of Samson's defeat, the Philistines held a great celebration with more than 3,000 men and women in attendance. During the celebration, the Philistines brought Samson out to perform and obviously gloat over his humiliation. They sadistically wanted to be *entertained*. However, no one noticed that Samson's hair had grown again. He asked God to strengthen him once more so that he might destroy the enemy. God answered his prayer. With his great strength restored, Samson pushed down the pillars of the temple. The roof collapsed, killing all inside, including Samson. In his death he fulfilled his purpose.

We don't know for sure if Delilah was there, but since it was a victory celebration of Samson's capture, it seems very possible the heroine of the hour would be present.

Perhaps if Delilah had turned to the true God, there would have been a chapter in the Bible devoted to her, as there was for Ruth. Delilah's weak character led her into all kinds of sin, and sin eroded her ability to love. It destroyed her, her family and those around her.

Let us allow her life to call us to be women filled with godly character. Let us commit ourselves not to be a constant dripping, but to be a constant encouragement to our husbands and to others.

Give in to God's Control

Delilah. The very name is synonymous with seduction and treachery. I would like to shrug my shoulders and say, "I can't relate." But truthfully, I can. My character was much like hers before I came into contact with the cross of Jesus.

The need to be loved and accepted, to have power and wealth were very strong desires that motivated many of my actions. I could well have betrayed a man to gain position or satisfaction or pleasure for myself. Of course, I never thought of myself as that cold or calculating, but looking back, I realize I could easily have gone in that direction.

s sexual manipulation, we also see deceit, emotional manipula-
greed in Delilah's life. Even though I gave up the outward sin, I still see some of Delilah in my heart. At times my emotions and feelings are so strong that I can choose righteousness only if I'm in line with God and his word. Satan sends powerful delusions, swaying and deceiving me through my emotions. I need the input of godly men and women to keep my perspective.

Even as a Christian, a wife can be destructive in her relationship with her husband. She can be critical of him. Perhaps his physical appearance has changed, maybe his spiritual intensity has lessened, or he's burdened by life's daily demands. It may be that he's grown so much that she becomes competitive or jealous. She may build him up, only to tear him down privately, in front of friends or, even worse, in front of the children.

I have blown it in all these areas. It's only when I have looked into the mirror of my own heart that I've been able to die to this behavior. The Lord has forgiven me and has been very gracious in all of my shortcomings.

We as women often struggle in the area of finances. Personally, I've manipulated or been deceitful in this area. Be it for a new dress or new furniture, my motto was "where there is a desire, there is a way." I've had to die to this behavior and to think responsibly. I've had to learn to ask, "What is best for us as a family?" and "What is best for the kingdom?"

God is loving and full of grace. He has given me an incredible husband, David. As my sin is wanting to be in control in all areas of my life, God has given me many loving people to help me repent and change. God has enabled me to build up and not destroy the man in my life. Giving in to God's control has blessed not only my marriage, but my children and ministry as well. I wish Delilah had known the God I know. I wish she had learned, as I have, that his way is *truly* the only way.

Coleen Graham
Burbank, California

 FOCUS Do you try to manipulate your husband or others to get what you want? Do you keep pushing until you get your way, or do you trust God to give you what is best in every situation?

12

NAOMI

BETTER NOT BITTER

Book of Ruth, especially 1; 2:1-2, 18-22; 3:1-5, 16-18; 4:14-17

During a period when Israel was led by the judges, a severe famine occurred. Forced to leave their home in order to survive, a family from Bethlehem—Elimelech, his wife, Naomi, and their two sons—went to live in Moab. Whatever previous hardships they may have faced, we don't know; but this one was surely difficult. Uprooted to live among strangers—and idolatrous enemies of Israel at that! But this was only the beginning.

Naomi's story really cannot be told apart from the story of her daughter-in-law, Ruth. Just as their hearts were linked, so were their future blessings.◆

A n arduous journey. An unknown destination in an unknown land. A radically different culture. That's what Naomi faced as she took her two sons and followed her husband to escape the famine in Israel. Elimelech had decided not to trust God for food and took matters into his own hands. Whether Naomi shared in this fateful decision or Elimelech decided alone, it turned out to be a portent of things to come. Much of Naomi's life was destined to be marked by tragedy—and by lessons learned from her own lack of faith in God's promises.

Whatever benefit came from their early move to Moab was obliterated by the unhappiness which followed. The tragedies that befell Naomi tested her faith—rather than bringing her closer to God, each seemed to drive her further from him and deeper into herself. The losses hit hard. How her heart must have ached! How many tears must have been shed! Naomi had found a land of plenty to satisfy their physical needs, but she neglected her spiritual needs and allowed her soul to become bitter.

The Journey Home

Bitter. That's how Naomi described her feelings as she and her daughters-in-law discussed their circumstances: "It is more bitter for me than for you," she told them, "because the Lord's hand has gone out against me!" (1:13).

It's not hard to understand how Naomi came to feel this way. She was left to face a terrifying situation: alone in a foreign land and responsible for her two daughters-in-law. The society's laws and customs were far from kind to single women. How would they live? She had little resources and few options. But she had faced tragedy before and survived. She was a resourceful person, capable and courageous. But in feeling so alone she mistakenly thought it all rested on her. She let her bitterness close her heart. Sadly, she was losing touch with the true source of strength and sustenance.

In desperation her thoughts turned to her homeland. Even after all the years, her memories of the land around Bethlehem were vivid: fields of wheat and barley waving golden in the sun, vineyards ripe with succulent grapes, groves of fragrant olive trees. When word came that the famine was indeed over, Naomi did not hesitate—she was bound for home.

The three women set out on the homeward journey. But Naomi had second thoughts about what she was requiring of Orpah and Ruth. How could she care for them when she had no security herself? And who knew what kind of reception these "enemy" women would receive in the land of Judah? Their best possible future would be to remain in their own country, returning to their mother's house young enough to marry again. So she generously gave them her blessing and released them from any obligation to stay with her. "May the Lord show kindness to you, " she declared, "as you have shown to your dead and to me."

It was a bittersweet moment. Naomi's assessment of the situation was all too real, but so was the love among them. They had been a family for a long time and Naomi's influence had been a significant factor in the other women's lives. Her daughters-in-law wept and kissed her. They protested. But Naomi insisted. Orpah turned back. Ruth, however, was determined to go with Naomi. She was willing to give up her homeland, to travel with Naomi, to care for her and even to adopt her religion. Naomi had obviously inspired a deep devotion in Ruth.

The irony was that Ruth, who had obviously learned of God from Naomi, was the one who exhibited trust. In the years of isolation from her community of believers, Naomi may not have forgotten God, but she *had* forgotten his promises. In her darkness, she had become short-sighted; she had lost hope. Ruth, however, had caught a glimpse of the light, and now it was her faith that lit their way.

They traveled together north to the southern edge of the Jordan River, crossed Jericho into Judah and on into Bethlehem—about a five-day trip.

It took a great deal of courage for two women alone to make this trip. Depending on each other, they became even closer. Naomi surely turned to God and prayed for protection on their journey. Ruth had no idea what lay ahead. But there was a youthful excitement in her anticipation of the unknown.

"Can This Be Naomi?"

Naomi's arrival at home created quite a stir. Her friends easily could see the changes that time and tragedy had wrought. Her neighbors whispered among themselves, "Is this Naomi?" Surely they saw the pain and bitterness etched into her aging face. In her frustration Naomi cried, "Don't call me Naomi. Call me Mara (*bitter*), for the Almighty has made my life very bitter" (1:20).

Naomi lashed out and blamed God. "The Lord has afflicted me;" she said, "the Almighty has brought misfortune upon me" (1:21). In the face of tragedy, Naomi, like so many of us, turned bitter rather than turning to God. We can so easily forget that God's promise is not for a life of ease, of plenty, or a life without pain. His promise is to give us his grace—grace sufficient to sustain us whatever comes. And often our suffering is a consequence of our own decisions—something we easily forget, just as Naomi seemed to forget that she and her family left God to go to the foreign land of idolaters. When Naomi cried out, "I went away full, but the Lord brought me back empty," she was not only speaking of the loss of the family she loved, but of the loss of her relationship with God.

Gratefully, the story doesn't end here. We may give up on God, but God doesn't give up on us, and he didn't give up on Naomi. God is faithful. He had a different future in store for Naomi—one she could not have imagined. In Naomi's darkness, God's light showed through.

God Restores Hope

At home in Bethlehem, Naomi and Ruth's problems were far from over. Perhaps the beauty of the countryside made the humble white-washed home in which they lived seem less barren, but the fact is Ruth and Naomi were very poor, and they had very little food. Fortunately, they had arrived as the barley harvest was beginning, and Ruth offered to glean sheaves left in the fields for the poor.

Boaz, a wealthy relative of Naomi's husband, was a man of standing in the community. He was impressed with Ruth's hard work, her commitment to Naomi and her faith in God. No doubt he was also embarrassed that he had done nothing about Naomi's plight, while Ruth, a foreigner, had been so devoted to her. From then on, Boaz saw to it that Ruth had extra food and protection from the reapers.

Of course, Naomi was pleased that Boaz had taken such an interest in Ruth. Through him Naomi's hopes for the future were reborn. Being aware of the custom of *go el*, she devised a plan to bring Ruth and Boaz together. *Go el* was a law of the Israelites that allowed a close kinsman to marry a widow, and then the first son born would inherit the former husband's property. It was a risky plan. There was actually a closer relative who had the right to marry Ruth, and since she was a Moabite, the custom might not have been honored at all. But Naomi believed that Boaz was the right man for Ruth, and she guided Ruth toward him. She explained to Ruth the custom of lying at Boaz's feet to let him know she was available. Out of her respect for Naomi's judgment, Ruth followed the advice even though it must have seemed strange to her. Together they took a risk, using the ritual to their advantage, and trusted in God and Boaz to work it out. Naomi's faith had been nurtured and was blossoming once again. She was trusting in God and actively pursuing a better future in keeping with God's will.

God's design for their lives was realized, and Naomi's dream came true when Ruth and Boaz were married. Naomi's friends rejoiced with her and declared that her daughter-in-law was "better than seven sons." The true love and mutual respect of Naomi and Ruth was clear to all. Led by Naomi, Ruth developed a genuine faith and trust in God, one that allowed these women to support and sustain each other.

It's a Boy!

What happiness it was for Ruth to be able to lay her newborn son in his grandmother's lap. What happiness for Naomi to hear the women around her declare, "Praise be to the Lord....He will renew your life and sustain you in your old age" (4:14-15). Naomi laughed with joy. An old woman who had given up in bitterness now experienced life anew.

This is the fabulous promise of God: At any moment his grace is available to us and our lives can become new—whatever our ages or circumstances. And what better proof of that than a grandmother's joy in caring for a beloved grandchild. Miraculously for Naomi, her empty, bitter heart was now filled with love. Her faith was renewed, her hopes restored. A bitter woman became a better woman—one blessed by the God of all grace.

Finding New Dreams

Naomi and I really have a lot in common. Had we ever met, we could have identified with each other quite easily. When I was 30 years old and the mother of two young children, I traveled to Japan, a country with a very different culture, one where people worshipped idols. I know the loneliness of being away from all that is familiar, the continuous struggle to keep my faith strong. After establishing a church and a Christian camp, we were forced to return home by an illness that left me in traction for most of a year. Just as Naomi discovered, life does not always go as planned. I asked God over and over why I had to be in that situation. I know firsthand the temptation to question God.

Many years later, we once again found ourselves in Japan, hoping to stay there this time. But after I suffered a broken hip as a result of being caught in a subway door, we were again forced to return home.

We settled in San Diego where God used us to teach and counsel. I dreamed of long years together in San Diego, frequent trips to Japan, rejoicing together in seeing Japan evangelized. But God had a different plan. After three months my husband, George, was diagnosed with acute leukemia. With great faith he accepted his imminent death. I tried hard to accept it, but in my heart I asked *why. Why now?*

Becoming a widow, thus being single again after 51 years of marriage was very difficult. Again and again I reminded myself of Romans 8:28. It wasn't easy. My constant and steady companion gone, my daily life turned into a daily struggle. Every night alone, every mealtime a reminder of my solitary life. No longer involved with other couples for dinner or fun, I found myself wishing God would take me also. Why was I still here? I didn't seem to fit anywhere. My dreams of a life for myself were gone. Like Naomi, I know the battle to rebuild your life when the one you shared everything with is taken away, and the life you had built together is stripped away.

But God is faithful! My daughters and grandchildren were a great support. I was welcomed as a regular member of families in both San Diego and Japan. I made four trips to Japan in the first year and found again the ways I was needed.

Fulfilling ministries opened up to me with both older women and spiritually single women—a fruitful field and such a blessing. I am thankful for the joys of being with supportive, sustaining women of faith and of teaching my faith to others.

Just as Naomi rejoiced in her grandchild, I am hoping now to live to hold a *great-grandchild* on my lap.

Life will always bring us times when we don't understand—as it did to me and to Naomi. But from experience I know God is in control, and if we stay strong in our faith, blessings will follow.

Irene Gurganus
San Diego, California

What is your first response to trials in your life?
How does God want you to face difficulties?
If you trust his promise, how will the trials affect you?

13

RUTH

DREAMS CAN COME TRUE

Book of Ruth; Matthew 1:5

A little nation on the shore of the Dead Sea, Moab was not a significant threat to Israel, though they were never on friendly terms. Their uneasy relations began during Israel's exodus to Canaan. Because of Moab's animosity, God later instructed his people, "Do not seek peace or good relations with them as long as you live" (Deuteronomy 23:6).

The nation's beginnings were shameful. Moab was the son of Lot's daughter, born to her after she got her father drunk and seduced him (Genesis 19:37). Almost a century later, the idolatry of the Moabites was particularly eclectic. In addition to their own god, Chemosh, they worshipped the gods of many other nations.

One might not expect anything wholesome or beautiful to come out of a place like Moab, but Ruth, the Moabitess, is that bright star. God chose to tell her whole story in a book that bears her name.♦

Famine. A dreaded word. A word that brought a sense of helplessness and fear to Elimelech and Naomi and their sons. Leaving their homeland of Israel, they went to live in Moab. Shortly after their arrival, Elimelech died. Naomi's two sons married Moabite women, one being Ruth, even though God's standard was for Jews to marry fellow Jews so their faith would not be weakened (Jeremiah 13:23-27; Ezra 10:1-4). This new, mixed family had 10 years together, then Naomi's two sons died, leaving young widows.

What would happen to Ruth? Did God have a destiny for a woman who was the "unbeliever" in a mixed, 10-year marriage, widowed in her 20s, childless, and left to take care of a forlorn, widowed mother-in-law? Ruth's life had overwhelming challenges. What had she learned from her new family about the one God? How would she respond to her challenging circumstances?

God-Centered Goals

Making a difficult decision, Ruth speaks powerful words of devotion, warmth and concern for Naomi from a God-centered heart (1:14-18). "May the Lord deal with me, be it ever so severely, if anything but death separates you and me" (1:17). Having been impacted by her new family's faith, Ruth's God-centered perspective inspired intense loyalty toward an increasingly bitter and hurting Naomi (1:13, 20-21). Ruth left her homeland determined to take care of Naomi. She chose to do what was right—no matter the cost. Certainly, she could have stayed in Moab, remarried and not taken on such heavy responsibilities. Enduring Naomi's bitterness, she didn't give in to the temptation to say, "I don't need this. I've got enough of my own sorrow to deal with." Having decided to go with Naomi, she faced many uncertainties during the 100-mile journey—a rough one for two women to take alone, but God watched over them.

Upon their arrival in Bethlehem "the whole town was stirred" (1:19), scarcely recognizing Naomi because of aging and bitterness. She even wanted her name changed to "Mara," which means *bitter*, as opposed to Naomi which means *pleasant*. (Customarily, names signified a person's character—current or projected.)

In contrast, Ruth had a positive, solution-oriented spirit. Needing food and a livelihood, Ruth willingly offered to do the lowliest of tasks. She worked hard in the fields, following the harvesters and gathering the grain which was left behind for the poor. Starting in the morning, working steadily throughout the day, Ruth was quickly noticed. In fact, the whole Jewish community had been impressed by Ruth's devotion to Naomi (2:11-12).

Ruth "happened" to be working in a field belonging to Boaz, a distant kinsman of Naomi's husband. God's practical protection and loving guidance were evident in Ruth's life. She was very aware that she was a foreigner, an outsider, so she must have felt humble and a bit insecure (2:10, 13), but she responded forthrightly to Boaz in a gentle, endearing and expressive manner.

In an uncustomary move, Boaz invited her to join him and the harvesters for lunch. Ruth was not bashful; "she ate all she wanted" and saved some leftovers for her mother-in-law (showing her thoughtfulness). Continuing to work until evening, Ruth returned to Naomi with all her grain and leftovers from lunch, greatly impressing her mother-in-law. After hearing of Ruth's interactions with Boaz, Naomi began to scheme and dream for the daughter-in-law who had become like a daughter.

Ruth did not complain about her difficult and degrading work or her tiredness. Ruth was a hard worker not just a talker! She put her heart and energy where her mouth was. She was willing to do whatever it took to love and encourage Naomi during a difficult time in her life.

Radical Risk-Taker

As the dark cloud of bitterness began to lift, Naomi concerned herself with getting Ruth a husband. Her scheming and dreaming gave birth to a plan. She gave Ruth specific advice to take radical, yet appropriate, action according to the customs of that day. Naomi told Ruth, surely with a gleam in her eye, "Wash and perfume yourself, and put on your best clothes." She further instructed her to go to Boaz at night, where he would be sleeping on the threshing floor, and initiate for him to be her kinsman-redeemer (to marry her).

Ruth, who dreamed of marrying again, had a trusting, obedient spirit toward Naomi "and did everything her mother-in-law told her to do" (3:5-6). This was a potentially embarrassing and frightening situation. Ruth had to have courage and once again be a risk-taker for this marriage with Boaz to happen. She was willing to risk her reputation, her job and her life for her dream to come true. Because of Ruth's "noble character," Boaz was so honored by her vulnerability and boldness that he became protective of her reputation (3:11-14). He discretely, but eagerly set the wheels in motion to marry Ruth. She had won him over by allowing God to make her a woman who was loyal, hard-working, gentle, respectful, trusting, courageous, bold, humble, kind, giving, grateful and faithful to God in spite of being a "foreigner." During a time in Israel's history when "everyone did as he saw fit" (Judges 21:25), a young widow from Moab set the standard for integrity—God's standard. The atmosphere of faithlessness gave her every excuse to follow suit, but instead, she followed God.

Lasting Legacy

Thanks to Naomi's radical advice and Ruth's faithful compliance, Ruth and Boaz were married. Boaz, a godly and rich landowner, was highly respected in the Bethlehem community. Ruth, the poor widowed foreigner who once gleaned in his fields, became his wife. This unlikely, dream-come-true marriage was surely above and beyond the dreams that both Boaz and Ruth had for themselves (3:10 and 2:13). The powerful, loving God whom we serve blesses us when we persevere, faithfully obeying him—our dreams and beyond can come true (Ephesians 3:20-21).

In blessing upon blessing, "the Lord enabled Ruth to conceive and she gave birth to a son" (Ruth 4:13). Children are an incredible blessing from

God (Psalms 128:3). Ruth, a Moabitess, a Gentile, became the great-grandmother of one of the greatest earthly Jewish kings, King David, and then a direct ascendant to the King of Kings, Jesus.

Even as a daughter-in-law, Ruth's love and devotion to Naomi is credited by the community as "better than seven sons" (4:15). During this era, having one son was more highly esteemed than having many daughters. The above compliment to Ruth is fantastic! This commendation was precipitated by her love for Naomi. Because of this special love, Ruth is eternally remembered by a whole book in the Bible bearing her story and her name. Also, she is specifically mentioned in the direct genealogy of Jesus (Matthew 1:5).

Naomi was abundantly blessed through her relationship with Ruth. This deep, exemplary relationship brought renewal, joy and change to Naomi's bitter, empty life. God's grace worked this change through the powerful vehicle of the loving relationship of a daughter-in-law with her mother-in-law (one woman's love for another woman).

God says the greatest gift is love (1 Corinthians 13:13). God has lavished love on us with the sacrifice of Jesus for our sins. This incomprehensible love changes us to be more like Christ. We can say we "love," but like Ruth, our depth of love is evident in our actions, our loyalty and sacrifice to meet people's needs. Just imagine the incredible impact women could have on the hurting, "harassed and helpless" world if there were more *Ruths*—women who have God-centered goals and who are radical risk-takers! May God help us to love like Ruth!

Grateful Not Fearful

Being born in Cuba and leaving immediately after the revolution to come to America when I was four years old made me a *foreigner*. I remember the fears and insecurities—the same ones that Ruth must have felt. All this shaped my personality, causing me to be cautious and guarded about whom I would trust. I only trusted and felt comfortable with my immediate family.

Growing up in the '60s and '70s, I dreamed about helping women to be successful, to be totally secure in who they were, to ensure equal rights and opportunities. I got serious about the Bible and living for Christ when I was 17. God has truly helped me, a foreigner, to feel secure in his love and to realize my dream to help women through the incredible teachings of the Bible.

Also, like Ruth, God called me to be a radical risk-taker. I have never liked the word *coward*, and yet it is in my nature to hold back and be fearful, to be cowardly. As a brand-new Christian, I was afraid of speaking about God before groups. I did not feel comfortable talking about spiritual or personal issues, but I knew that to be like Jesus I needed to speak up about the truth. By decision, prayer and support from others, I conquered these fears.

God continues to test my heart and to call me to overcome fear. Going and doing what seems dangerous or foolish in the eyes of men is a constant challenge as I serve God. Living by faith and not by sight. Not giving in to hysterical fears as my husband and I share the gospel around the world. Love for God and people's souls enables me to rise above the fears and temptations to be cowardly.

Several years ago we spent time in a Middle-Eastern city in order to build up the church. We came in for a summer with our family after all the other Americans were expelled for evangelizing. I overcame my fear, and God blessed us with fruit and kept us safe.

As my husband, Kip, and I went into Moscow, the capital of the then Communist Soviet Union, to start a Christian church, I felt those *foreigner* insecurities once again. But, God had given me a purpose and a mission, like my sister of old, Ruth. He wanted me to love like Ruth loved and to show that love to the oppressed women who had not been given a chance to learn about God or the Bible. I didn't speak Russian, but I prayed hard to meet bilingual people. God answered my prayers and continues to build my faith as we see so many modern day miracles happening in the Russian churches.

Even staying home has tested my fear level—since home is the Los Angeles area. Drive-by shootings, gang violence, the terrible April riots of '92, the arson fires of '93, the blatant prejudice, the worldliness, and most recently, our 6.7 earthquake and aftershocks that we are still experiencing at this writing—all these tempt me to be fearful for our three children. I pray daily for God's direction and protection in their lives. We are in L.A. for God to work through our lives! Like Ruth, God has made many dreams come true for us, and like Naomi, many bitter people with whom we have shared the gospel have changed.

God has given me a *Boaz* in my fantastic, godly husband. Our lives have been full of adventures, joys, blessings as well as challenges over the last 20 years. I'm thankful that God will give us, along with all other disciples, a "lasting legacy" since our names are written in his book of life. We can give others the incredible opportunity to have this *lasting legacy* as we realize *God-centered goals* in our lives, as we deeply love others as Ruth loved Naomi, and as we are *radical risk-takers* boldly sharing our faith.

Elena McKean
Los Angeles, California

 Do you have God-centered goals for your life? Are you willing to be a radical risk-taker to see those goals realized?

14

HANNAH

1 Samuel 1, 2:1-26

Joshua, the mighty military commander, had led Israel into Canaan and had exacted the widespread surrender of the Canaanites. After his death, God appointed judges as spiritual counselors and military leaders. This system of leadership set them apart from other nations, who were ruled by kings, and made a statement to the world that the nation of Israel had a different kind of monarchy with God himself reigning as their king. The exploits of the judges can be found in the book of the same name with the exception of one, the last judge, Samuel.

Of all the judges, Samuel's biography is the most complete. When Israel grew envious of the pomp and splendor of royalty in the nations around them (the very nations they were to have destroyed), they coveted a king of their own. God was disappointed but granted their request; thus, Samuel played the leading role in the transition between the judges and the kings.

The importance of the role God chose for Samuel to play was significant enough for the Holy Spirit to tell Samuel's story beginning before his birth. Samuel was set apart by God to have a special birth to a special mother with a special faith. His mother's name was Hannah.◆

Hannah was a most fortunate woman. A woman blessed far beyond many women of her time. She had a home of her own and a compassionate, generous husband named Elkanah. A man of strong character, he worshipped God and led his family in sacrifice. During a time when a woman was considered blessed if she was not abused or thrown out of the house at the slightest whim of her husband, Hannah could bask in her security.

But Hannah had even more. Elkanah loved Hannah—far more than he loved his other wife, Peninnah. This love led him to show favoritism toward her—openly, for all to see. At the time of sacrifice when he gave meat to each of his wives, he gave Hannah a double portion. Elkanah wanted his beloved to be happy, even though she was childless.

Frustrated, he tried to understand the tears of his wife. He beseeched her, "Hannah, why are you weeping? Why don't you eat? Why are you downhearted?" (1 Samuel 1:8). But Hannah could not be comforted. God had closed her womb. Above all else, she wanted a son. Having a son would elevate her in the eyes of her husband and her people. She would have a legacy, her children's children.

Year after year, this sad, childless woman suffered. To add to her misery, her rival had both sons and daughters, and she seized every opportunity to flaunt her good fortune. As Peninnah paraded her brood around for all to make the comparison, anger must have risen in Hannah's chest, tightening her throat. Every time she heard the buzz around town, *the good news*, "Peninnah is pregnant again," she must have felt a stabbing pain in her heart. She had to wrestle with what she thought was obvious: Peninnah was more favored by God than she.

She Was Taunted

Hannah's response to Peninnah's taunting was to weep bitterly. Seeing Peninnah nurse her newest baby boy, Hannah must have felt the ache of her heart and the emptiness of her arms. What emotions and temptations did she have? Anger, jealousy, inadequacy? Whatever she felt, her strength of character would not allow her to retaliate or discredit Peninnah. It would have been easy. Hannah knew she could influence her husband; she had his ear. He was concerned for her. She must have been tempted: *Play on Elkanah's sympathy. Beg him to stop Peninnah's taunting. Have him send her away. After all, isn't that how Sarah dealt with Hagar's mocking?*

Year after year nothing changed. The trips to Shiloh became more and more unbearable. Each trip reminded Hannah that her biological clock was ticking. She was so depressed she could not join in the celebration. She could not eat.

The years of suffering had taken their toll on Hannah, but the pain had also created in her a strong resolution. She searched her soul. *What would it take to change God's mind? What could I put before him to prove my earnestness? A vow?* Hannah petitioned God as never before. If God would give her a child, she would give him up. She would give him back to God. There would be no turning back. "Would I be able to do it?" had gradually been transformed into, "I will do it!"

A decision of faith. One that can only be made by a woman possessing unwavering trust in God. She put herself and her child completely in

God's hands—under his control. Hannah's faith is even more remarkable when one considers the moral decadence of the day. Hannah was surrounded by flagrant disobedience. Even in the house of God, Eli's sons were desecrating the temple by ignoring God's instructions for sacrifice. Hannah believed in the power of God Almighty and was not weakened in her faith by the hypocrisy of others.

Her God did not change. He was the same God who above all hope, gave Abraham a son in his old age. "O Lord Almighty, if you will only look upon your servant's misery and remember me, and not forget your servant but give her a son, then I will give him to the Lord for all the days of his life, and no razor will ever be used on his head" (1 Samuel 1:11).

A completely humble request. No undertones of "I deserve." Hannah placed herself before God as a servant who was begging to be remembered. She believed that if God did answer her plea, the response would come from his righteousness, not hers. It would be a gift—not a right.

She Was Accused

As Hannah talked to God she did not speak aloud. Praying for God's ears alone, Hannah was ahead of her time. Her prayers were completely internal. For the most part, the Israelites believed that the value of petition lay in words—loud and many. Hannah understood that prayer is communion with God, heart to heart. Hannah didn't say prayers, she poured out her soul to God, assured he was listening.

Eli saw her lips moving and instantly assumed the worst. Harsh and accusing, he marked her as a woman who mocks God. Eli was more harsh with Hannah than with his own sons who flagrantly slept with such women. A woman of lesser conviction and strength would have slipped away—unwilling to defend herself against a priest.

Out of a pure heart toward God, Hannah responded with humility to his anointed, "Not so my Lord. I am a woman who is deeply troubled. I have not been drinking wine or beer; I was pouring out my soul to the Lord. Do not take your servant for a wicked woman; I have been praying here out of my great anguish and grief" (1 Samuel 1:15-16).

Touched by her earnestness, Eli stopped questioning and responded with tenderness and certainty, "Go in peace, and may the God of Israel grant you what you have asked of him" (1 Samuel 1:17). To be in the presence of such devotion to God must have challenged the one who was to be God's man to the people.

She Was Vindicated

Jesus would later say, "If you ask believing, you will receive" (Matthew 21:22). Hannah understood. Leaving the temple, she washed her face and was no longer sad. She had been through a time of trial, but she was no longer downcast. She went home, made love with her husband, and waited for God to do what he had promised.

Her misery did not lead her into sin. Now, not only was God going to grant the desires of her heart, but she was a stronger and more appreciative woman as a result of her struggle. She had proven her noble character.

She bore a son who never compromised before priests or kings. He led God's people with the character born in his mother. With his strength, he united a crumbling nation, broken by ungodly leadership and willful sin. The ark was returned to Israel and the Philistines subdued. Samuel anointed the first king of Israel and later confronted him with his sin against Jehovah.

To the Israelites he spoke as they forgot the Lord:

> As for me, far be it from me that I should sin against the Lord by failing to pray for you. And I will teach you the way that is good and right. But be sure to fear the Lord and serve him faithfully with all your heart: Consider what great things he has done for you (1 Samuel 12:23-24).

God knew he had a servant in Samuel, for such was his mother.

Faith Not Sight

Hannah is my sister. I relate to her. God's decisions for her life often pierced her to the core and tempted her to ask, *Why?* Such has been the last six years of my life.

Why did God allow my husband, Calvin, to die so young? He was only 48 when cancer ate away his body and took his life. I watched my youngest son, Joseph, only six, grieve over something he could not comprehend. I listened to his cries at night, "Mom, I hurt. My body hurts all over." Then came the nightmares. How can someone so young deal with that level of grief?

Yesterday he became a teen, growing up without the much-needed guidance of a father. The temptation is always there for me to be angry with God, to feel punished.

When I think about the faith Hannah showed when she took her young son to Eli to raise, I am challenged. From a worldly perspective, Hannah made a foolish decision. After all, had Eli not failed with his own two sons? Would he not fail with Samuel?

Her faith teaches me that God makes the difference. He made the difference in Samuel's life when he began speaking to him while still a boy, teaching him lessons on obedience. The visual aid was Eli and his sons.

God is making the difference in Joseph's life. From a worldly perspective, he has scars that were expected never to heal. The world does not know that God can heal any scar.

"'For I know the plans I have for you,' declares the Lord, 'plans to prosper you and not harm you'" (Jeremiah 29:11). You see, Calvin's death did not negate God's promise. Just as God kept his promise to Hannah, I see his hand in Joseph's life. Joseph has become a young man who loves God and loves people. One of his teachers recently told me about watching Joseph help a girl in his class pick up her books when all the other children were laughing. She was touched.

Two months ago a young father in our church died, leaving two young daughters. As Joseph reached out to these little girls, he showed a level of compassion few other children could feel. To be able to help others because he feels so deeply has helped heal his scars and made him happy.

As I reached out to the young widow, I understood how she felt. My suffering has value, for what I have learned through it all I can teach others. Calvin isn't here to give me advice or to teach Joseph needed lessons, but God is discipling both of us. We miss our husband and dad, and it hurts to have lost him. But God meets our needs: "I have plans to give you hope and a future" (Jeremiah 29:11).

Joyce Conn
New York, New York

 FOCUS
Do you trust God is still with you even when life brings you disappointments and hurts?

15

MICHAL

ALL OR NOTHING

**1 Samuel 14:49-52, 16, 18, 19:1-18, 25:43-44;
2 Samuel 2; 3:1-21, 6:1-23**

One day as Saul, the first king of Israel, sat on his throne, an inconspicuous shepherd boy rose to international fame. David had killed Goliath. Saul showed him proper gratitude and honor initially—at least outwardly. But in his heart Saul felt neither true loyalty nor obligation to the man who had saved his country from the Philistines.

Saul's growing pride in his power had driven God to reject him as king. God would allow another man the honor of the lineage of kings. Saul was not submissive to the will and sovereignty of God. His desire was to circumvent God's plan and to stay in power. Saul's faith had eroded to the point that he had forgotten how futile it was to fight against God.

David had been anointed, but secretly. However, his overwhelming popularity caused Saul to suspect that God had chosen David to be king.

David was the darling of Israel. Probably a great many women were swooning over this valiant young warrior-hero. One of those women was King Saul's own daughter, Michal.◆

She was a teenage fairy-tale princess. Her father...the king of Israel. Saul was powerful, fabulously wealthy and the anointed of Jehovah God. Her husband...the champion of the Israelites, slayer of Goliath. David was a handsome, accomplished musician, adored by men and especially by women. As a teenager, Michal was living every woman's dream.

Not much is written directly about this woman and her life but, it is obvious that she was a woman of influence by birth. She was then *influenced* by the three key men in her life: David, Jonathan and Saul. As in our lives today, Michal had to make choices in response to these influences—choices which ultimately determined her final destiny.

She Chose a Man After God's Own Heart

"Man looks at the outward appearance, but the Lord looks at the heart" (1 Samuel 16:7). These were the words that God spoke to the prophet Samuel as he was searching for the man who would succeed Michal's father as king of Israel. Samuel, the spiritual leader, was first struck by David's oldest brother, Eliab. He said, in effect, "What a MAN! Surely he's the next king!" But God said, "Hey Samuel, he may be handsome and tall, but don't be deceived by that. I want heart!" Then Samuel met David. He could *smell* him before he saw him. The Bible says that he was "ruddy and handsome"—a shepherd boy straight out of the Eddie Bauer catalog. Samuel must have thought, *Lord, he's kind of short and. . .phew!. . .that's some kind of smell. Are you sure, Lord?*

God was looking deeper than the surface. He loved David for his heart. Is that what first attracted Michal? She must have heard of David following his incredible showdown with Goliath. He had gone to the battlefront to bring some cheese sandwiches to his older brothers. Had Michal encountered him before he killed the giant, she wouldn't have given him a second glance. The entire Israelite army and King Saul were quaking in their sandals at the huge Philistine's taunt to come and fight. Seized with indignation and the power of God, David stepped out and felled this monster with his slingshot! What a great victory for God's people and for David, God's man. Michal's brother, Jonathan, was deeply moved by David's faith and courage, and they became "one in spirit."

Was Michal looking on, breathlessly, as her brother and father brought David to the palace to serve in Saul's army? I can picture her watching him and listening to him as he played and sang to soothe the king. By the time David had declined to marry her older sister Merab, Michal was head-over-heels in love. The servants were the first to notice. It was only a matter of time before Saul knew. She was a woman *after* David's own heart!

She Chose to Be Loyal

Even before David killed Goliath, Saul's rebellion, among other sins, was destroying his ability to lead God's people. In 1 Samuel 16:14 the Bible says, "Now the Spirit of the Lord had departed from Saul...." Twisted by his hatred and jealousy of David (1 Samuel 18:7ff), Saul was intrigued by his daughter's love for David. He saw it as a perfect opportunity to kill David. He set the price for Michal's hand at 100—not dollars or shekels but Philistine foreskins! A diabolical plan. A disgusting task. Saul hoped that David would be destroyed in his quest. Michal must have been horrified by her father's actions.

However, David and his compatriots were victorious and killed double that number of Philistines. Saul's plan was foiled, and Michal became the wife of David. The whole situation only reinforced and intensified Michal's love for her new husband. Michal was forced to choose: to please her father was to lose her husband. At this point it was no contest. Undoubtedly, Michal was also influenced by her brother's intense loyalty to David. Jonathan did his best to reconcile his best friend and his father, but only a brief cease-fire resulted.

In 1 Samuel 19:9-10 the drama reached a climax as Saul made a personal attempt on David's life, hurtling his spear at him in rage. David escaped to his wife's arms, and Michal arranged for his escape from Jerusalem. As David ran for his life, loyal Michal stayed behind to face his pursuers.

She Chose to Be Ruled by Fear

It is a pity that Michal's story could not end at this point. The truth is that hers is not the happy-ever-after tale it started out to be. As Saul gave in to fear and rebellion toward God, unfortunately, so did his daughter. As David escaped into the night, the soldiers at Michal's door grew impatient. Perhaps they threatened her. When her father arrived, she opened the door. In the bed was not the ill and sleeping husband they had expected, but an idol dressed up to trick them. Her deception exposed, Michal faced an angry king who wanted answers. Her heart was racing; her hands were sweating, and her fear ran rampant over her loyalty. Her resolve to defend David crumbled under her father's hateful gaze, and she lied, saying that her husband had threatened to kill her if she had not let him escape. She did not realize that one lie would change her present, her future and her eternity. Scholars believe that King Saul acted on her statement as David's desire to nullify the marriage. Shocked as events unfolded, but afraid to tell the truth, she soon found herself married to another man whom her father had chosen. She had, in fact, made a choice herself—security over truth, safety over loyalty.

Michal was with Paltiel for 14 years, and in time, she apparently became a good wife to him. One can only imagine the regret and bitterness buried deep within Michal's heart. After the death of Saul and Jonathan, David made an agreement which would cement his claim to the vacant throne of Israel. One of the prime conditions was that his estranged wife, Michal, be given back to him. She must have been in considerable turmoil, having been asked to switch her marital loyalties once again. We do not know for sure what David was thinking. Perhaps he had truly loved her all those years even though he had taken several other wives during their separation. We know also that having the daughter of Saul as his wife further strengthened his succession ᴛᴏ ᴛʜᴇ throne. Whatever the reasons, Michal found herself once again in the palace of the king–this time, *King David*.

Michal's bitterness finally spilled out of her heart in 2 Samuel 6:16-23, her final recorded encounter with David. It was an incredible day of victory for the youngest son of Jesse. Not only had he become king, but the ark of the covenant was finally being brought back to Jerusalem! As the ark entered the city, Michal spied her husband leaping, dancing and praising God. She must have thought something like, *How unbecoming, how unlike a true king. Saul would have never acted like that!* The Bible says that she was not merely embarrassed, but that "she despised him in her heart" (2 Samuel 6:16). She was truly a bitter woman. What biting and critical words she said to her husband, a man after God's own heart, "How the king of Israel has distinguished himself today, disrobing in the sight of the slave girls of his servants as any vulgar fellow would!" (6:20).

David responded tersely in rebuke of his wife: "It was before the Lord, who chose me rather than your father or anyone from his house when he appointed me ruler over the Lord's people Israel–I will celebrate before the Lord. I will become even more undignified than this, and I will be humiliated in my own eyes. But by these slave girls you spoke of, I will be held in honor" (6:21-22). How sad that in the end Michal's fear and jealousy, like that of her father Saul, destroyed her impact on God's kingdom. The very vulnerability which she despised, she so desperately needed. She died childless and bitter because she allowed ungodly influences to dictate her choices. The woman who had it all ended up with nothing!

Choices That Count

I was sobered by studying the life of Michal. The time I "spent" with her challenged me to realize that the course of my life is determined by the decisions I make. It is crucial to consciously choose the right things every day and not just to "let the chips fall where they may," hoping it will all work out.

My first resolve was *to renew my commitment to godly influences.* This principle was a critical part of my growth as a young Christian. It seems that many choices were clear-cut then. I chose to love God more than my family, my friends and my feelings. Today, after more than 15 years as a disciple, the choices seem a bit more fuzzy. It is easy to let the influence of the world creep into my life and lower my spiritual standards. As a middle-aged woman, I am tempted to become satisfied with my commitment to God, to my husband and kids, and to those who are lost. Of course, all other commitments take root in my deepest commitment—to love God with all my heart, soul, mind and strength. As I read about Michal, I realized there was no reference to her relationship with God. Though she had grown up with the *anointed of God,* she was not exemplary in her devotion to God. I believe that Saul's lack of heart for God was transferred to his daughter. I want to love God not only with my actions, but with my heart so I can influence my children to do the same. I must commit myself daily, all day, to being *a woman after God's own heart* and a woman led by God's word and God's people.

Second, I have resolved *to renew my commitment to be grateful.* At this moment I feel that I am the most blessed woman in the world. I have a great husband (Marty), two loving children (Ben and Maria), people like Kip and Elena McKean, Bruce and Robyn Williams, and Al and Gloria Baird as faithful friends and co-workers, an incredible church—and that is just for starters. I need to remember daily how blessed I really am, and that will keep me out of a bunch of trouble! Michal's gargantuan lack of thankfulness destroyed her marriage and her life. That makes me want to choose gratitude over grouchiness every single day.

I thank you, God, for Michal and the things I have learned from her through the Word. Although she lived thousands of years ago, her choices are the same ones I have to make today.

Chris Fuqua
Los Angeles, California

FOCUS

Are you known as a "woman after God's own heart"? Are you ready to get rid of anything that blocks this desire in your heart?

16

ABIGAIL

1 Samuel 25:3-42, 27:3, 30:5; 2 Samuel 2:2, 3:3; 1 Chronicles 3:1

King Saul had chosen to lead Israel *his* way, not God's way. It was Saul's rejection that caused God ultimately to reject him as king. He knew that God had annointed David, but that did not cause him to relinquish his throne. On the contrary, Saul chose to fight God's decision by embarking upon an obsessive mission of personal vengeance to eliminate David.

Saul turned his military forces away from fighting the enemies of Israel to pursuing his own personal enemy, David. David never fought back; he simply ran for his life. David ran to caves, to foreign cities, even to Israel's worst enemies. Along the way, he gathered hundreds of loyal volunteer followers, among them, many brave fighting men.

Although David's men would have liked to kill Saul, David never allowed it, but held valiantly to his integrity and his dependence on God's decision and intervention. While David was running for his life, narrowly escaping Saul's murderous pursuit, he and his men came to Maon. They met some shepherds there who were watching the vast flocks of a very wealthy man named Nabal.

David, the former shepherd, greatly impressed Nabal's servants by the protective and courteous treatment he gave them while he was in their neighborhood. So when David and his men had a serious need, he expected reciprocal hospitality, but Nabal rudely refused. His wife, Abigail, however, had a different heart and character.◆

What will I be when I grow up? Will I marry? Who will I marry? Will I have children?

These are questions pondered by young girls today as well as in the days of Abigail. A child who grew up to be an "intelligent and beautiful woman" would have had these questions (1 Samuel 25:3). She would have had the imagination to dream of betrothal to a wonderfully handsome, strong and kind man. One who would adore her and be respected at the city gate.

Yet, who materialized as this man of her dreams? Nabal, the bully. A man who was "surly and mean in his dealings" (25:3). A man of whom his servants would say, "He is such a wicked man that no one can talk with him" (25:17). Abigail was dealt a challenging life situation. Once married to this ill-tempered man, she showed a strength of character that overcame difficult circumstances instead of being overcome by them.

Adopt an Attitude

Abigail had to choose the attitude with which she would live each day. She could be miserable, full of self-pity, a discouragement to those around her. After all, she faced insensitivity day in and day out.

Or, she could choose to be bitter. *Why did God allow this to happen to me? It is his fault. I do not deserve this. And Nabal, that fool. He has ruined my life. What if I had married someone else? I would be happy then. How could any human being be so horrible? Perhaps I would feel better if I made him miserable, if I punished him with the cold shoulder, sharp glances, terse words, apathy. I should make him pay.*

She could live each day hoping it would be different. *He's smiling this morning. Maybe today will be different.* Yet, when he never changed, she could have become depressed. *I had hoped things would be different. Isn't that faith?* When her expectations let her down, she could have chosen to be cynical about life.

Abigail had a tough situation and could have chosen any of these attitudes. Let us look at the character and actions which enabled her to overcome this difficult situation.

Opt to Overcome

Grapes were drying or being pressed into juice that was poured into skins. Sheep were hanging, being dressed for dinner. The smell of roasting grain mixed with the aroma of loaves and cakes baking. This is the backdrop in 1 Samuel 25 as Abigail was busy working and organizing the women around her.

Abigail accepted her lot in life and was making the most of it, instead of being unproductive and surrounding herself with self-pity and regret. She could have authored the phrase "God grant me the patience to accept the things I cannot change, the courage to change the things I can change, and the wisdom to know the difference." There was no change on the horizon for her situation, yet she was making her life productive.

The second way Abigail overcame her difficult situation was that she took help from others. She would have remained in ignorance had she not listened to her servant who explained what Nabal had done and what David had planned. Often others can give us information, advice or scriptures that we would not know without their help. Abigail is an example of a wise woman because she let others help her.

Abigail was also a positive thinker. She overcame her tough life situation by having an attitude of "let's see how it can be done." In verse 17, the servant says to Abigail, "Now, think it over and see what you can do..." There was an expectation that Abigail would do something that would make a difference.

Think about the situation. A king with four hundred men against one evil man. How tempting it would be for Abigail to resign herself to the obvious outcome, thinking she could make no difference. She believed her life *could* make a difference—even in a seemingly impossible situation. The women around Abigail caught this spirit of initiative as they quickly responded to her plan and went on ahead of her. Abigail's attitude influenced the lives of those around her. They, too, had become women of initiative, courage and faith.

Hate to Hesitate

Abigail believed that *sooner was better than later*. How often great faith, good intentions and high ideals get buried beneath mounds of procrastination. Abigail overcame her circumstances by being urgent. She "lost no time" (v 18). She moved "quickly" (vss 23,33,42). David told Abigail that if she had not acted quickly he would have done great harm.

When we are dealing with people like Nabal, who are difficult and sinful, do we realize that the root of the problem is that they are in need of a Savior and a complete character change by God? Do we act quickly, like Abigail, to help them learn how to be made right with God? Or do we think that there is always more time? If Abigail had waited, it would have been too late.

Persevere with a Plan

Abigail combined initiative with personal responsibility. She took action to solve the problem. She did not wait for someone else *out there somewhere* to do it. She went to David and took the blame for her husband's behavior. This showed great humility and opened the door for mercy from David. She was willing to risk her life to help someone more undeserving. Only a humble heart, taught by the heart of God, could have done this. She did not know how David or Nabal would respond to her. Yet, she knew that following God meant personal risk. She had the courage to step out in faith in the face of great risk and the lack of support from her husband. It takes courage and persistence to go alone and keep doing good without encouragement from those close to you. But it can be done. Abigail did it. Nothing stopped Abigail. Does anything stop you?

When we are caught up in circumstances beyond our control, we often become caught up in self-pity also. The best offensive against self-pity is a good plan of action. Look at what you can do, not at what you cannot do. Look out for the needs of others who need even more help than you. This is what Abigail did.

Bring Out the Best

Perhaps the most important aspect of overcoming her difficult situation was Abigail's dependence on God's truths. Though David was a powerful man, she boldly called him to the future and his accountability before God. In verses 26-31 she pleads with him not to repay evil for evil. She brought the best out of David, calling upon his desire to be faithful to God's truths.

But how do we show good judgment and dependence on God as Abigail did when the pressure is on us? Do we follow Abigail's example of firmly establishing God and his standards as the priority in our lives? Do we think ahead to practical ways we can put this principle into practice? Abigail's priority led her to good judgment. Her good judgment brought the best out of someone. Poor judgment and timing can tempt even the good-hearted to do wrong in reaction. Abigail took the time to consider how to stir another up to love and good deeds (Hebrews. 10:24). She was also convinced that David, striving to follow God, was full of goodness (Romans 15:14). Then she helped to draw that goodness out in him. Do we, like Abigail, bring out the best in other people?

Reap a Reward

God did not forget Abigail, and he will not forget you. Abigail was rewarded for her righteousness and courage. In the same way, if we cultivate the good character traits which help us overcome problems, we will be rewarded. If your husband is not a disciple, it may mean that if you persist in your example, he will become a new person in Christ. Or it may mean that you will grow in your character and become more like Christ because of overcoming a challenging circumstance. The circumstance, like Nabal, might never change, but if we continue to do good and grow in God's grace by the power of God, one day we will hear, "Well done, good and faithful servant! Come and share your master's happiness" (Matthew 25:21).

Never Give In or Give Up

I am an idealist at heart. I like everything to turn out "happily ever after." I want to know that the movie will end okay before I pay money to watch it.

Yet, time and time again, I see injustices in life. Some are physical and some are situational. Yet I know that God loves each person individually and that every injustice in life brings the opportunity for the light to shine and for God to be glorified. I have known that for a long time, and yet I remember well a particular *Nabal* in my life whom I allowed to cause me to lose faith and become bitter and cynical.

My husband and I had not been in the ministry long and were seeing God work powerfully in many people's lives. We were in a small traditional type of church. I assumed that everyone in the church, especially the leaders, would want to see the church grow and would pour their lives into that task. We worked hard, my husband preached the Word, and we gave our hearts to the people.

What a shock it was to discover one day that a leader in this church was standing in the back as people left, handing out materials full of lies and prejudices against us. My faith waned, my anger grew, and I stewed inside. *Why did this happen?* We were trying our hardest only to be "slam dunked." Hatred started to grow in my heart. Cynicism started creeping in, and I became somewhat aloof and apathetic. My husband had been hurt. I had been hurt, and it was not fair.

I had to wrestle in my heart with the things I was feeling. I watched my husband respond with honesty, but not bitterness. He had decided to respond righteously. I read the Scriptures and hung on to the ones about the kingdom of God and God's faithfulness, even when people are faithless. I thought about Jesus on the cross and his incredible forgiveness and wondered if I could do that.

As I think about Abigail, I realize how close I came to living a life of bitterness, retaliation and cynicism when confronted with a *Nabal* in my life. Her life inspires me to see unfair situations in a different light. I have seen many *Nabals* in my life and others' lives since that time. I am determined to be like Abigail and trust God and never give in or give up.

I have already experienced great rewards. I have the privilege of seeing the kingdom of God that I read about in the Bible lived out in flesh and blood. I see unity forged, and I look forward to an eternity with my father in heaven.

Jeanie Shaw
Burlington, Massachusetts

 When you are tested by a difficult situation in your life, do you act righteously and quickly?

17

TAMAR

OVERCOME BY EVIL

2 Samuel 13:1-32, 14:27; 1 Chronicles 3:9

King David had brought his nation to unity and peace. He had won their hearts and loyalty by his bravery on the battlefield. With success came the luxury of leisure. Having conquered all major foes who might have proven a threat to his kingdom, he could stay home and send soldiers out under the leadership of his commander, Joab, to fight the remaining minor battles.

David had several wives, many children, abundant wealth and time on his hands. Idleness led to lust, which led to adultery, which led to murder....What about his family during his hours of spiritual darkness?◆

David had many daughters, but Tamar was the only one mentioned in the Bible. She was beautiful and unmarried. We know that Israelite girls were married by 12 years of age during this time, so Tamar was probably very young when we first meet her.

Her brother, Amnon, was consumed with sexual desire for Tamar. Not only was she beautiful, but she also had integrity and strength of character. Taking advantage of Tamar's virtue, Amnon plotted to seduce her. He pretended to be ill and asked to have Tamar care for him. Their father, unaware of the deceit in Amnon's heart, granted his request and sent Tamar to his room.

The Incident

In her innocence, Tamar served her brother, feeding him with her own hands. She trusted him as most young girls trust their older brothers. Trust produces vulnerability. Tamar let down her guard and willingly surrendered herself emotionally to Amnon. Feeling comfortable in his presence, she joyfully prepared a meal at his bedside. As Tamar reached out her hand to serve him, Amnon grabbed her and pulled her into his bed.

One of the greatest fears in every woman's life is to be overpowered by a man who forces sex against her will. It is especially devastating if she is a virgin. Her most intimate part is exposed, fondled and violated.

Tamar knew this moment would change the course of her life forever, and she began to beg him to spare her. She appealed to his integrity, his heart, his compassion, but it was too late. The rape was over, and the torment had begun.

The Hurt

We will be hurt over and over again in this lifetime. People we love will be taken away; people we respect will disappoint us; someone we trust will betray us. Deep scars are produced that apart from a relationship with God have no way of being resolved or healed.

The type of hurt that Tamar experienced was the personal devastation of sexual abuse. In the place of innocence there was now shame. Often the assaulted woman believes it is her fault. Usually she has been told not to tell anyone, possibly even threatened if she does. Deceit seems the only way to take away the shame and protect what little sense of innocence remains. Deceit easily takes root in the heart and begins to migrate like a malignant cell into every relationship. She will even begin lying to herself to block out the pain and with it, the ugly memory. The greatest devastation, however, is the loss of personal integrity, the degradation of a woman's self-image.

The tragedy was intensified for Tamar by the reality that her abuser was her brother—someone she had trusted, someone who should have been her protector. The devastation of the violent attack was worsened by Amnon's subsequent response of hating and humiliating her: "Get up and get out!" he said to her. Calling his personal slave, he said, "Get this woman out of here, and bolt the door after her" (2 Samuel 13:15,17). Violated and dismayed, Tamar left hating herself.

Amnon's sin devastated this innocent girl's life. It is not fair; it is not right for one person to act destructively toward another, but it goes on every day.

The Response

In the violence of the rape, Tamar's heart was changed. She walked into Amnon's bedroom pure, innocent, naive, a woman of integrity and character. She left disgraced and desperate. What a tragedy for a young life to be destroyed. But did it have to be?

> Do not repay anyone evil for evil. Be careful to do what is right in the eyes of everybody. If it is possible, as far as it depends

on you, live at peace with everyone. Do not take revenge, my friends, but leave room for God's wrath, for it is written: "It is mine to avenge; I will repay," says the Lord. On the contrary: "If your enemy is hungry, feed him; if he is thirsty, give him something to drink. In doing this, you will heap burning coals on his head." Do not be overcome by evil, but overcome evil with good (Romans 12:17-21).

It is not the abuses, disappointments and sorrows that harden our hearts. It is our response to these things. Most women have been involved in sexual experiences that have resulted in shame, but nothing compares to the horrendous violation of sexual abuse. Years later, the pain can still seem unbearable, and many women live as if the abuse is ongoing. The reason for this lingering pain is that women have allowed themselves to be overcome by the evil that has happened to them rather than overcoming the evil with good.

Tamar realized immediately what her future held as a result of the rape. She could never marry because she was no longer a virgin. She would never enjoy the laughter of her own children or the gentle touch of a man who loved her. She tore the ornamental robe worn by virgin daughters of the king as a symbol of a life torn apart by sin. She wept aloud in sorrow and pain. She secluded herself and became dependent on Absalom, her other brother. Although Absalom loved her and was willing to kill his own brother for her honor, Tamar's heart did not change. She remained a desolate woman the rest of her life (2 Samuel 13:20).

Many women wear the torn robes of shattered lives. Resentments that grow into bitterness and self-pity eat away at their character and their souls. Those attitudes produce deep, debilitating scars. If we allow them to continue, they provide fertile ground for all kinds of emotional destruction and illnesses. Tamar allowed it to go on too long in her heart, and her character decayed into that of a desolate woman with no future or hope.

The greatest test of our faith and dependence on God comes when something unfair is happening to us, something we did not choose. Throughout history God's people have faced false accusations, seen their children tortured, and suffered in countless other ways. Through all of that, God's standard has not changed. His expectation is wholehearted devotion to him—no matter the circumstances. It is that devotion that will rescue our hearts from any evil. To be able to overcome evil, we must surrender our hearts to God and do what is good.

We do not hear any more about Tamar. Amnon was murdered, and Absalom went on to betray his father, the king of Israel. Evil overcame the good in Tamar's family, and it overcame her as well.

The Healing

There could have been a different story written about Tamar. To retaliate and stay angry is easy. To separate yourself from people and not face the hurt is protective. To continue to lie to others and yourself is a good cover-up, but it is the wrong way to think. Had Tamar gone back to her roots, to the God of her people, her story would have been very different. God helps us to go from a wrong way of thinking about our hurts to the right way of thinking. He can help us to make sense out of the confusion and pain. Tamar never made the turn because she did not take captive her thoughts and then transform them into spiritual thoughts. Training our thoughts to be spiritual takes decision and discipline (2 Corinthians 10:4-5; Philippians 4:8-9).

Tamar needed to learn to forgive, not to hate. Although in some circumstances it may seem impossible to forgive, for Tamar, as for all women who have been sexually abused, the only way not to be overcome by evil is to forgive the abuser and the people who did not protect you. Forgiveness changes the direction of our hearts and, ultimately, our lives. To forgive allows us to put things in proper perspecitve—God can wipe away the tears and replace the painful memory with a deep sense of peacefulness. He restores our dignity.

Just imagine how Tamar could have affected her family and the history of God's people. In a family where there was jealousy and hatred, she could have inspired love and forgiveness.

What about our response to the bad things that have happened to us? Is there bitterness, resentment, distancing from the people who have hurt us? Tamar made the wrong choice. If like Tamar, we have made some wrong choices to the pain we feel inside, God can turn the weeping into dancing and the shattered dreams to joy. In response to hurt, let God sort out the feelings as you wrestle to make your thoughts godly. Think spiritually, respond out of a pure heart, and you will ultimately be overcome by good.

Good Not Evil

I was raised in what society would call a *dysfunctional* home. No one was on drugs or dependent on alcohol, but we suffered intense emotional abuse. I was told from the time I was a child that all the problems in my family were my fault, and I believed that because I had a tender heart then. Each of the four children protected themselves in different ways— my way was to fight back and take control. Any trust that was left in my young heart was destroyed before I was nine years old. I was sexually abused by my grandfather who was living in our home. He was suffering from a nervous breakdown and abused me over a two-year period in my parents' bed.

My response today when I am hurt is like Tamar's. I want to pull away and be hurt inside. I always feel responsible. It has made it very difficult for people to build relationships with me because the fighting and the pulling away communicates a response which is very different from what is really going on inside, which is anger toward myself. The sin is self-pity.

My response to sexual abuse was not to tell anyone what happened to me *and* not to trust anyone in authority. I did not ever want to be put in a position that would allow someone to have that kind of control over me. It has taken a long time for God to readjust my thinking and for me to learn to overcome the evil response of my heart with a good response.

I talk about the abuse now and get the help I need to work through the feelings. I am realizing that God is powerful, and I do not need to fear people or to even fear myself. To heal the scars and turn the sorrow into joy means a wholehearted surrender to God. At times it is a moment-by-moment decision. If I do not walk closely with God every day, my heart can quickly turn and be overcome once again with self-pity.

To prevent further hurt, Tamar withdrew from the people she had loved. I have also done this in my family, especially with my only sister. We have both been hurt by the abuses that happened to us, and we have built up tremendous resentments toward each other. But after praying faithfully for the last two years, God has changed my heart and hers. In just a few weeks, we will be seeing each other for the first time in 20 years. Susan and I are just starting to feel the relief of wounded hearts that are being mended by God. Rebuilding this relationship is just the beginning for me to learn to trust and to forgive.

Whatever has happened to you that still hurts, make the right choice and surrender yourself to God. His way is the way of good, and he is powerful enough to overcome any evil.

Shelley Metten
Los Angeles, California

FOCUS

When someone says or does something to hurt you, what is your response? Do you want to retaliate or to forgive?

18

QUEEN OF SHEBA

SHE CAME, SHE SAW, SHE BELIEVED

1 Kings 10:1-13; Matthew 12:42; Luke 11:31

After King David's death, his son, Solomon, established his reign in Jerusalem. Solomon's request for a discerning heart to govern God's people wisely so pleased God that he added to that gift of wisdom, the gifts of wealth and fame.

God opened the windows of heaven to pour these blessings into Solomon's life, and the world had never seen anything like it! Solomon became a genius: renowned statesman, architect, botanist, zoologist, ornithologist, author, poet, songwriter, teacher, highway engineer and military strategist. He spent 20 years constructing two of the most opulent buildings the world has ever seen: his palace and the temple of God. Rare woods were intricately carved and overlaid with gold. Fine fabrics were embroidered. There were jewels, along with ivory, gold and other precious metals. His wealth was staggering. But this was not a monarch living in luxury at the expense of an impoverished nation: "The king made silver as common in Jerusalem as stones ..." (1 Kings 10:27). He ruled over a happy, prosperous, secure kingdom. 1 Kings 10:1 says that the Queen of Sheba heard about the "fame of Solomon and about his relation to the name of the Lord."

"Men of all nations came to listen to Solomon's wisdom, sent by all the kings of the world... " (1 Kings 4:34). One monarch sent no representatives to return with a report—she came to see for herself. ◆

The Queen of Sheba came bringing gifts and asking questions (1 Kings 10: 1, 2, 10). She is one of only three Old Testament women mentioned by Jesus. He held her up as an example of one who spared no effort or expense to pursue wisdom. Think what she would have missed had she not made the sacrifice. She came. She saw his wealth, his influence and his friendship with God—and she was overwhelmed.

She Was Drawn to Solomon

Two entire chapters tell us the things we would all admire about Solomon (1 Kings 8, 9). As I read and reread these chapters in an attempt to understand what drew the Queen of Sheba to meet Solomon, it became clear that, at least at this point in his life, Solomon appreciated God and his power. Solomon's prayers reveal his heart and his understanding of God. Solomon praised God's reliability: "Not one word has failed" (8:56). He understood God's power to "turn our hearts to him" (8:58). Solomon's relationship with God was sincere and truly heartfelt. He wanted all the people of the earth to know the Lord and to have hearts fully committed to him (8:60). He understood our need to be forgiven by God—because we are all sinful (8:32-34). He knew that God knows each of us individually and that God not only gets involved in each one's life (8:32), he also punishes and rewards each individual uniquely (8:38-40). Because Solomon understood these concepts, God could use him powerfully. I believe that the Queen of Sheba was drawn to Solomon because of his dynamic, powerful relationship with God, and she made the sacrifice to travel "from the ends of the earth" to learn about his God (Luke 11:31).

She Was Overwhelmed

The Queen of Sheba was a woman of great wealth, courage, initiative and confidence. She made the journey to see Solomon, brought lavish gifts, and was confident enough to "test" him, yet she was overwhelmed. Why? Though it is not specifically stated, it seems that it was Solomon's wisdom and relationship to God which were overwhelming to her. Speaking to Solomon, she says:

> How happy your men must be! How happy your officials, who continually stand before you and hear your wisdom! Praise be to the Lord your God, who has delighted in you and placed you on the throne of Israel. Because of the Lord's eternal love for Israel, he has made you king, to maintain justice and righteousness (1 Kings 10:8-9).

These are very passionate words. Over and over in the book of Proverbs, Solomon states that wisdom comes from God only. At this point in Solomon's life he was very close to God and in touch with God's power, wisdom and authority. Solomon's devotion, evidenced by his wisdom, was both inspiring and "overwhelming" to the queen—overwhelming because, relatively speaking, she knew so little about God.

The queen was a responsive woman of passion and a leader by nature. When she saw what she lacked, she began to learn about God. She wanted to give back to God and to Solomon (1 Kings 10:9-10). She was convinced that God was God and Solomon was his chosen leader. She had never experienced anything like this! There is definitely power in the life of a person devoted to God.

We have probably all met someone who left us "overwhelmed." When we worship with a dynamic church and begin to know the people, we can be overwhelmed. Everyone seems so far ahead of us spiritually. They seem to be people *with no problems*. Truly the difference between believers and non-believers is that through God and his disciples, the believers have answers for problems and the power to confidently and joyfully proceed with life.

Solomon and the Queen of Sheba probably always remembered the spiritual heights of their time together. The friendship and the learning about God must have lifted them both higher. The Queen of Sheba is shown to be powerful, insightful, wealthy and, most importantly, a spiritually-minded woman. She encountered God and a man of God and returned to her country filled with an understanding she would never have gained had she not come to see for herself.

Overwhelmed by the Presence of God

I remember the first time I worshipped with a group of people who were excited about knowing God and about being a part of his kingdom. For many years I had been eager to please God and to "worship in spirit and in truth" (John 4). When I finally met with a group of Christians who were truly devoted to God, I was so overwhelmed that I wept. I believe that these were the feelings of the Queen of Sheba—"praise be to the Lord your God," she said (v 9). God was present. God was all around. God can be stunning, overwhelming, awe-inspiring. That was my reaction.

Now, I still have those feelings when I hear songs of praise to God sung by believers around the world. In my travels I am privileged to hear songs in different languages. The sounds are different; however, the spirit is the same—awe-inspiring and, at times, overwhelming. Yes, I can relate to the Queen of Sheba.

I also remember a devotional that my son Douglas led after returning from his freshman year at Duke University. Something had changed him. His message was inspiring. I had never heard anything similar to it, and like the queen, I had many questions. Later, I heard Kip McKean speak God's message powerfully from the Scriptures in a way that was moving and motivating, but I was overwhelmed and, again, had many questions:

How can I submit to God?
How will I balance family, job and total commitment?
As a woman with worldly position and power, how can I use all
    my talents for God to advance his cause?

Yes, there were many questions, but all had answers. While searching for those answers, I was challenged by the lives and the examples of Kip and Elena McKean and my son Douglas. The memories of those days and those discoveries remain fresh in my heart today.

My prayer for all my spiritual heroes and for you and me is that we never give in or give up—that is how Satan wins. We must always remember those "overwhelming" beginnings and allow them to inspire us to stay faithful, to travel the distance to the end of the journey. Our example, Christ, overcame potential sins of hatred and bitterness as he was overwhelmed with sorrow on his way to the cross. It is my prayer that we will overcome every sin that tempts us and finish as Christ finished.

Pat Gempel
Philadelphia, Pennsylvania

 FOCUS

How overwhelmed are you with God's blessings, with his wisdom? What are you willing to do in order to know him better?

19

GOMER

GOD'S VISUAL AID

Hosea 1, 2, 3

Golden calves were in place as the national gods of the northern kingdom, Israel. For 200 years it had been governed separately from Judah. Idolatry escalated as the gods of surrounding nations were adopted. Cult prostitution, witchcraft and human sacrifice became common. Baal, Molech, Chemosh, Dagon and others rivaled Jehovah for Israel's devotion.

A heartbroken God watched as his beloved flaunted her unfaithfulness before him. A long-suffering God put up with this deplorable spiritual adultery for 240 years. He sent prophet after prophet to beg Israel to abandon idolatry and return to the arms of the God who had cherished, led, protected and adored her. A faithful God sent one last prophet 70 years before the captivity from which there would be no return. That prophet's name was Hosea. For 40 years he powerfully called Israel to repentance. His most powerful visual aid was his own life and his marriage to Gomer.♦

We are not usually eager to learn about godliness from an adulteress. But God gave Gomer to Hosea so he, Israel and we could learn from her. As she was unfaithful to her husband, running after lovers of her sinful choice, so Israel was unfatihful to her God. As she represents God's unfaithful people, we can all relate. But Gomer specifically was a *wife*, and those of us who are married can learn from her unrighteousness how to be righteous. From one who brought hurt and shame to her husband, we can learn to bring joy and encouragement to our husbands.

Worldliness

Lust of the eyes. Appeal of the flesh. Worldly thinking. Mmm. That feels good and smells good and tastes good. Feelings so strong that we easily give into them. We say that we would *never* cheat on our husbands, and yet how quickly it can happen to any one of us if we are not careful. Just like Gomer, we can see and feel the enticing pull of Satan.

Nothing obvious. Just a look at a man. But then it turns into another look, and then a stare. Or, maybe, it's an innocent conversation. But, it turns into many more conversations, and you find yourself looking forward to having those conversations. You get a "good feeling" about it. Maybe he says things that make you feel good and build you up. Maybe you just like the attention. There might be sexual vibes or the selfish enjoyment of being treated like a queen. Gomer (and Israel) felt the same way (Hosea 2:5b). Satan has just begun his plan. And you have fallen into his "web of lust." If you don't get out *now*, you are headed straight for adultery.

Many of us would be tempted to look down on Gomer for her adultery, and yet, we could fall into this same trap tomorrow. Don't be self-righteous. Be sobered and be aware (1 Peter 5:8). It can happen to anyone!

Selfishness and Manipulation

Selfishness. Ugh! We hate to see it in our lives! And yet, we can be so much like Gomer. Selfishness was the motivating factor in Gomer's life. Her selfishness led her into adultery and kept her from being the supportive and loving wife she needed to be. She thought only of *her* needs.

Hosea, a devoted husband, had already given her so much, as God had given Israel (2:8). And yet, she wanted more! She was so consumed with her own desires, that she forgot what Hosea had provided for her. We can become so consumed with the things we want, that we forget the things we have. We've been given so much! Those of us who are married should be grateful. There are women who would love to be in our shoes. We need to thank God for our husbands.

With selfishness comes manipulation. Gomer and Israel were both true manipulators as we see in Hosea 2:7. Each would return to her beloved only if she was not getting what she wanted where she was. The goal of selfishness is to get whatever one wants. No one else matters. And, the adulterous wife could make herself seem penitent and respectful: "I'm going back to my husband!" When, in reality, she really just wanted pleasure for herself.

Can we relate? Oh, yes. We have learned how to get the things we want. We know how to say it, when to say it, and how much to say! We know how to get our way without even thinking about pleasing our husbands or denying our desires. We know when to cry, when to be sexy, and when to act like a helpless little girl. We can use all of these ploys at just the right moment to manipulate our husbands into giving us what we want. Much of the time we do not even realize what we are doing.

Hosea loved Gomer, and yet, she took advantage of his love. How many of us have husbands who want to please us, and yet we are *always* the ones being pleased? Rarely are their needs and pleasures met.

In the end, selfishness will only hurt us. Gomer was bought back by Hosea. She could have been a slave or prostitute. Or maybe Hosea paid off her new male companion to get her back. Anyway, it was far from being a glorious life for her. Her own selfishness had carried her to rock bottom. And no one is happy on rock bottom. The more selfish we are, the more unhappy we are. The more we give to others, the more we will be happy.

Hurt and Disrespect

Gomer had a *gift* for hurting Hosea. She knew how to do it, and she did it often. She had one child with Hosea and then two who were not fathered by him (God refers to them as children of unfaithfulness). At God's instruction Hosea named the last two children Lo-Ruhamah, *not loved,* and Lo-Ammi, *not my people.* Hosea was obviously distraught over the unfaithfulness of Gomer. Her actions did not build up and encourage her husband. On the contrary, they hurt him deeply.

But, how often do we do the same thing to our husbands? We say things that hurt them. We don't build them up with our comments (Ephesians 4:29). Our husbands get their feelings hurt more than we may realize. We can do severe damage to them with just one sentence. We must think before we open our mouths. Will this help or hurt?

Gomer obviously did not respect Hosea as the husband God gave her to lead and to love her (Ephesians 5:22-33). Her actions showed she only respected her feelings. No wonder their marriage was a mess!

If we don't respect our husbands, it is direct rebellion toward God. He has a specific plan for marriage: *Wives respect your husbands. Husbands love your wives.* There is no need to be insecure or feel like someone is more important than anyone else. We all have our roles. We are all the same in God's eyes. But, God's plan works best! We can choose to be disrespectful and hurtful toward our husbands and have a weak marriage. Or we can choose to be respectful, encouraging wives and have a great marriage that brings us happiness and brings glory to God!

Unsupportive

How does it feel not to be supported by the one you love the most? Not to be able to trust your closest friend? How enjoyable is it to be concerned about what your mate might do or say? This is what Hosea's life was all about! Gomer was unsupportive, unreliable and unpredictable. Gomer was more burden than support. He had to take time to bring her back home. He gave her chance after chance to repent and to change. He even had to take care of two children that were not his own (Hosea 1:6-9).

We are either true "helpers" for our husbands (Genesis 2:20), or we are hindrances. How often do they waste their energy being concerned about us. Concerned that we will not be able to handle daily pressures, that we might break like fragile china at the least little *bump*. Or, maybe, we are like bulls in a china shop. Our husbands fear we will try to take charge, control situations and speak out of turn. Which are you?

Gomer was married to a prophet of God. But that did not seem to matter to her. She did not care about his dreams or his mission in life. She cared only about herself. What more could Hosea have done for God if Gomer had been supportive and been a helper to him? What greater things could he have accomplished? Thankfully for Hosea, God used a difficult situation to teach his truth.

What about our husband's dreams? Do we even know what they are? Many husbands are held back from great accomplishments for God because of selfish and unsupportive wives.

We need to make decisions of integrity. Gomer never really decided to change. She continued in her sinful patterns day after day. Her faithful husband spoke the words that we need to hear:

> Who is wise? He will realize these things.
> Who is discerning? He will understand them.
> The ways of the Lord are right:
>   the righteous walk in them,
>   but the rebellious stumble in them (Hosea 14:9).

Let's walk and not stumble. And let's not give our husbands reason to stumble.

Giver or Taker?

I saw so much of myself in Gomer's selfishness. I had already made great strides in this over the years, but this study made me see how very much more I need to change!

I rely so much on my husband, Clyde. Honestly, I focus too much on his meeting my needs. I need to become much more of a *giver* instead of a *taker*. Sometimes it is a matter of dying to myself and pleasing him. Other times, I allow the needs of others to take precedence over his needs. I must trust God to help me take care of all my responsibilities. God will bless me if I put my husband's needs before mine, even if I am busy doing good things. Of course, these are areas we need to communicate with each other about. We have to all work together to meet family and ministry needs. But what I am talking about is not having an independent heart and being aware of Clyde's needs.

Just like Gomer, it is hard for me to deny my feelings and desires—even if those feelings and desires are righteous. I must remember and trust God's plan for me as a wife to be a "helper." I have seen over and over that when I obey God, I am happier.

I am seeking more than ever to do all the little things that meet my husband's needs. These little things add up and show him my love and respect. Consider these "helper" questions and responses: "What would you like to do?" "How can I help?" "What would make this easier?" "What else can I do?" "Sure, I'll be glad to do that."

My 15-year-old son, Spencer, is very much like his dad. He is always ready to help anyone who needs him. Recently, Clyde was sick, and I was convicted because Spencer was so much more supportive than I was. I had much more of an attitude like Gomer—selfish and concerned about what I could not do because he was sick. I hated seeing that attitude in my heart, and I really wanted to change it. Gomer helped me to see my selfishness and to realize how it can really hurt my husband.

God is very patient with all of us. I am so thankful he gave me this opportunity to see the changes that I need to make in my life. In the spirit of 1 John 4:20, I see more clearly than ever that I cannot be grateful for a God I cannot see unless I am grateful for a husband I can see. And I am!

Jane Whitworth
Ridgewood, New Jersey

 FOCUS Are you a burden to your husband in any area? In what areas are you a support?

20

WIDOW OF ZAREPHATH

FROM FAMINE TO FAITH

1 Kings 17:7-24; Luke 4:24-26

Sin. Repentance. Or doom to come. The message of the Old Testament prophets came to turn God's people around. He wanted to spare them the destruction that would surely come if they continued in their disobedience. As the Hebrews turned away from God to worship idols, God allowed them to test the power of their chosen "gods" to save them from the surrounding nations who coveted their land and their manpower.

The prophet Elijah was sent with an unpopular message to an especially hostile audience: King Ahab and Jezebel. They wished him dead from their first encounter. To establish his God-given authority, Elijah explained to Ahab that there would be neither dew nor rain for the next few years except at Elijah's word. The ensuing drought and famine sent Elijah on his own adventurous journey, first to a brook in the Kerith Ravine where he was fed by the ravens, then on to the town of Zarephath in Sidon. There a courageous widow provided for his needs.◆

It was a morning like many others. She had the same heavy-heartedness that seemed to be a part of every day in Zarephath. Sadness, hopelessness, deadness seemed to accentuate the dry, famine-parched land. There had been no rain for a long time.

She decided to gather sticks as usual to make a small breadcake, blocking out the reality that it probably would be their last bit of food. She and her young son walked together to the gate to find the sticks they needed for a fire.

Her eyes teared every time she looked into her son's eyes. They were so trusting as they gazed into hers. And yet she could do so little to prove worthy of that trust. Since his father had died, they only had each other, and they missed his providing for them. The famine seemed to be drying out their hearts as well as the streams.

The Request

A curious thing had occurred of late. A command from the God of the Israelites had been made known to her. The command was that she was to supply food to a man of Israel. She wondered what Israelite would come to the homeland of Jezebel to be supplied with food. As they walked toward the gate, her mind drifted from thoughts of kings and queens back to famine, to food, to sticks, to the son she loved so much.

Just as they arrived at the gate and began gathering their sticks, a strong voice asked, "Would you bring me a little water in a jar so I may have a drink?" She looked up into an unfamiliar face; it was not the face of a Sidonian. *Could this be the one?* she thought.

As she went to get the water, a second request came. "And bring me, please, a piece of bread." Unbelievable! She stopped dead in her tracks. How could this stranger be asking her to give the sum total of all the provisions she had left for her and her son?

Command or no command—this was too much!

A Decision to Trust

We do not know much about the first meeting of the prophet Elijah and the widow. The details are sketchy. However, the impact on both of their lives is tremendous, and the progression of their faith is a challenge and encouragement for all people for all time!

This account of the unnamed widow and her son provides us with insight into the mind and heart of God. She had no heritage that would have taught her to "give all that she had" because of faith in the one, true God. On the contrary, the worship of Baal was promoted in her country. This pagan widow would be an unlikely candidate for God's favor—at least in the mind of a Hebrew prophet.

As a Sidonian woman, even her initial response to Elijah was not one of belief but of recognition. She said, "As surely as the Lord *your* God lives, I don't have any bread, only a handful of flour in a jar and a little oil in a jug. I am gathering a few sticks to take home and make a meal for myself and my son, that we may eat it—and die" (1 Kings 17:12). She did not sound very hopeful of a blessing from God.

At first glance, we see a woman with an emotional reaction, facing the facts of her desperate situation. Any sentimentality on Elijah's part would have negated God's command, and therefore, the promise of God. Yet God was allowing an impossible situation to open this woman's heart to possibilities unknown to her and her son.

By first giving up *all* she had, she would experience the power of the one God—this in contrast to a hopeless plea to a lifeless Baal. Elijah saw past her reaction. He realized that fear had been her constant companion for

a long time. He began his request with the words, "Don't be afraid."
What went through her mind with Elijah's specific request?

> "Go home and do as you have said. But first make a small cake
> of bread for me from what you have and bring it to me, and
> then make something for yourself and your son. For this is
> what the God of Israel says: 'The jar of flour will not be used
> up and the jug of oil will not run dry until the day the Lord
> gives rain on the land'" (17:13-14).

He said *first*—put him first. He called for this priority of action with
a promise from his sustainer, *Yahweh*. Was it the man's forcefulness that
moved her to action? His sensitive understanding of her problem? Her
fear of *not* obeying this command?

All that we know is that she went away and did as he said. She met
the prophet's demand, and from that day forward there was food for her,
her family and Elijah. She experienced the provision of her need—a daily
miracle for more than three years.

A metamorphosis took place as a result of hearing the Lord and
obeying his command. With each passing day, her level of trust became
deeper. Learning to trust God is a daily decision. Words are easily
written and easily read, but life is an hour-by-hour challenge.

Taking It Higher

Years later, the progression of the illness and the death of her son must
have caused the widow to relive the hopelessness she had felt when she
first met Elijah. Fearing that the guilt of her own sin caused his death,
she cried out in anguish to the prophet (17:17-24).

What thoughts were racing through her mind as Elijah took him from
her arms and mounted the stairs to his upper room? Could she hear the
man crying out to God for the life of her son? How long she waited isn't
told, but it must have seemed like an eternity. Hearing the footsteps of
the prophet, she looked up, prepared for the worst yet hoping against
hope for the best. Elijah entered holding her son in his arms, her
breathing and smiling son. The prophet's words resounded joyously in
her heart as she held her child close, "Look, your son is alive!"

Her response came from her experience and her genuine conviction,
"Now I know that you are a man of God and that the word of the Lord
from your mouth is the truth" (v 24). Little did she know that her

example would be used one day by that same God's only Son as a challenge to the complacency and stubbornness of those who were religious rather than faithful.

No More Excuses!

Fear, distrust, anger and self-reliance. A description of my sinful nature. When challenged, I sometimes draw back and want to quit rather than to take the challenge and change. I might obey at first, but when I'm required to trust and do what seems impossible to me, I sometimes stop short and whine and whimper. Acting childish and immature, I pridefully believe that I know, more than anyone else, why I cannot be who I need to be. Without a daily decision to have faith, these faithless responses would rule me.

The widow of Zarephath challenges me in her example of faith while going through *real* adversity. She hesitated only slightly, and then gave *first* to Elijah, facing the facts of her situation. Amazing! The victories in this widow's life were even greater because of the extreme nature of both incidents.

I want to always remember to respond to God in trust no matter how extreme the situation might be. This was brought home to me as I watched our son Dan struggle to become a Christian. I was completely helpless and could only totally rely on God, believing and trusting that he would raise Dan from the dead, spiritually. And he did!

I have the privilege of having two close friends who were widowed at an early age. Seeing the challenges they face helps me to know some of what the widow of Zarephath would have experienced—especially during a famine and drought. To have lost a husband and father was difficult enough, but she was also facing the loss of her son.

God patiently brought her full circle from not knowing him at all to being a woman who was confident in his provision for her.

How often must an amazing act of God be waiting just around the corner, and I thwart it because I don't keep my emotions and fears under control. The widow really does take away all of my excuses. When I think of her story, I want more than ever to believe God and the *Elijahs* he puts in my life. Her life causes me to get tougher in the right way and expect more out of myself and others.

I'm so thankful that God demands that I be my best, yet is patient while I grow into the person he wants me to be. I'm so thankful for the *Elijahs* in my life who won't settle for anything but what God has commanded! Like the widow of long ago, I know that "the word of the Lord...is truth." And God will continue to help me to have faith in obeying that truth.

Debbie Wright
Ridgewood, New Jersey

 When you are in difficult circumstances, do you rely on yourself or on your God?

21

JEZEBEL

A HAUGHTY SPIRIT BEFORE A FALL

**1 Kings 16:29-33,18:16-19:2, 21:1-28;
2 Kings 9:30-37; Revelation 2:20-23**

God had given Israel what they asked for, a king—first Saul, then David, then Solomon. During the reign of Solomon, idolatry became so flagrant that God desired to take the kingdom away from him! But God had promised Solomon's father, David, that the throne would stay in his family. So God kept his promise, by taking only part of the kingdom away from Solomon. He divided the land north and south and gave the smaller southern kingdom to David's lineage.

Having their kingdom divided was to serve as a wake-up call for the Israelites—the problem is, they didn't answer the call. As shameful as their dishonor was, the Israelites continued to turn away from God. The southern kingdom (Judah) tolerated idolatry, and the northern kingdom (Israel) promoted it! All the idolatrous kings of Israel were bad, but the worst was Ahab. His evil was exceeded only by that of his Baal-worshipping queen. Her name 3,000 years later would still be equated with shamelessness and treachery: Jezebel.◆

T ake the greedy heart of Miss Hannigan in *Annie*, the power hunger of Ursula in *The Little Mermaid*, the vile cruelty of Cruella in *101 Dalmatians*, the murdering jealousy of the wicked queen in *Snow White*, combine them with the sexual perversion of a porn queen, and you have a character sketch of Jezebel, wife of King Ahab. Jezebel, however, was no fictitious character. She was as real as we are.

Without God at the center of our hearts, we too can become a *Jezebel*. She is femininity run amok!

Jezebel, the wife of King Ahab and daughter of King Ethbaal of the Lidonians, was the chief priestess of the false god Baal of Maleka.

Psalms 135:15-18 describes idols and their worshipers:

The idols of the nations are silver and gold, made by the hands of men. They have mouths, but cannot speak, eyes, but they cannot see; they have ears, but cannot hear, nor is there breath in their mouths. Those who make them will be like them, and so will all who trust in them.

In Jezebel's pursuit of Baal she became blind to God, empty in her boastful speech, deaf to the cries of others and eventually spiritually and physically dead.

Blind to God

We are all created with a true need for God (2 Peter 1:3-4). Idols offer a quick fix that temporarily fills the void but never fully satisfies. Jezebel continually shut her eyes to God and chose to be blinded by the immediate pleasures of humanism and idolatry.

The most dramatic example of Jezebel's blindness was at the showdown on Mount Carmel. Elijah told Ahab to summon all the people and the prophets of Baal on Mount Carmel. Interestingly, Jezebel was not there to see God's glory. Could it be that Ahab could not persuade her to go? Did she suspect the outcome and fear for her life or her public image? Maybe she did not want to expose herself to anything that might unsettle her belief system. In any case, Jezebel sought the comfort and false security of her own castle walls—walls that kept her from seeing the power of God.

Romans 1:20 tells us that God has revealed himself to us in many ways so that we are without excuse. God had revealed himself completely to Jezebel by demonstrating: 1) his authority by stopping the rainfall, 2) his power by responding to the sacrifice on Mount Carmel, 3) his righteous judgment by killing the prophets of Baal, 4) his mercy by restoring the rains, and 5) his loving patience by allowing Jezebel time to repent. In spite of all she witnessed, she chose to hide behind her walls, her arguments and her pretentions "that set themselves up against the knowledge of God" (2 Corinthians 10:4-5). She refused to be conquered and rescued by God.

Empty Boastful Speech

Jezebel wielded her tongue with power. When God withheld rain from the land, Jezebel tried to kill all the prophets of God. By getting rid of the messengers, she hoped she could escape God's purposeful discipline and that her words would go unchallenged. Meanwhile, Jezebel's prophets vainly beseeched Baal for rain for three years.

God proved that his words were full of power and her words were full of noise. At the spectacular day-long show of emotional frenzy at Mount Carmel, Jezebel's prophets tried in vain to awaken Baal's attention to their sacrifice. Elijah asked God to show himself to the people "so these people will know that you, O Lord, are God, and that you are turning their hearts back again" (1 Kings 18:37). Immediately, God's presence was displayed with a fiery blast that consumed the sacrifice, the altar, the wood and lapped up the water used to soak it. Elijah then commanded the people to kill the prophets of Baal.

The news of the death of Jezebel's prophets and God's victory incited her murderous vow to Elijah: "May the gods deal with me, be it ever so severely, if by this time tomorrow I do not make your life like that of one of them" (1 Kings 19:2).

Her determined vow sent Elijah running in fear. Only a serious one-on-one time with God and the companionship of Elisha helped replenish the courage of this devastated man. God knew her threats were empty, boastful words. Elijah needed convincing. God showed Elijah that his still, small voice was infinitely more powerful than Jezebel's vicious shrieking.

Deaf to the Cries of Others

Jezebel's pagan god of "Land and Fertility" demanded temple prostitution and the sacrifice of children. Jezebel obviously gave no honor to God because she had little respect for people created in his image. Blindness to God deafens our ears to the cries of others. Sacrificing children is as easy as cutting unwanted hair if they are seen as a few bones and skin cells. *Besides, her contribution to society was far more important than anything these children could contribute.* Children and needy people would only have complicated her personal goals and service to Baal.

How empty, sensual and degrading the worship services to Baal must have been. Perhaps we can picture a choir of temple prostitutes singing "What's love got to do with it?" A life without Jehovah God is a life without true love (1 John 4:7-18).

Jezebel was deaf to the soul-level cries of her husband. In spite of the unforgettable demonstrations of God's power, Ahab's heart was not turned to God. The greedy king desired the land of Naboth, but Naboth refused out of respect for God and his fathers (1 Kings 21:1-16). When Jezebel found her husband sulking and refusing to eat, she inquired, "Why are you so sullen? Why won't you eat?" Ahab pitifully related Naboth's rebuttal. Jezebel got frustrated with his indecisiveness and chided him for his wimpy attitude. She could not hear his cries as those of a man who needed to be called back to his God—because she never knew his God.

Jezebel took matters into her own hands. She would make Ahab happy by indulging his sinful nature. In a deceptive plan, she used two scoundrels to accuse Naboth of cursing God and the king. At the testimony of two witnesses, he was stoned to death. Temporarily Ahab was a happy man—until his *enemy*, Elijah, confronted Ahab with the truth of his wickedness and its consequences (21:20).

No Breath, Just Death

Jezebel's strong convictions for Baal and Ahab's wimpy convictions for God bore seed in their wicked sons. Out of Jezebel's stubborn rebellion, a woman who stood for *land and fertility* could only give her children land and *futility*. In her fertility she bore them. In futility she raised them. She did not nurture them or love their souls; she saw them born only to see them die in humiliation. She gave them land that was not hers to give, land that they could only die and rot on. Her children were sacrificed at her altar of self-worship.

Twelve years after Ahab's death, the prophet Elisha anointed Jehu to reign as the new king of Israel. His first duty was to rid the earth of Ahab's descendants. When Jezebel heard of Jehu's intent, "she painted her eyes, arranged her hair and looked out of a window" (2 Kings 9:30). Pride was such a dominating force in her life that it remained in control even as she faced her demise. Still trusting in herself and the image she portrayed, she readied herself to face certain death. If she was going to die, she was concerned only about having her face and hair right, not her heart. Or, possibly, for the first time Jezebel was seized with remorse and gave in to tears of regret and brokenness. If so, her pride closed her heart again, and she covered her puffy, swollen eyes with make-up—not wanting anyone to see her vulnerability.

Jezebel's stubborn, prideful heart could not allow her to face defeat and death in any way other than the way she had lived—flagrantly scoffing at God. Surrender and humility were too great a cost for her. It's a pitiful vision to see a woman pridefully and arrogantly walking up to the gates of hell. No matter the cost, she lived her life the way she wanted to—never bowing her knee to Jehovah God.

Pretentiously perched at her window, the queen publicly displayed herself, perhaps to intimidate Jehu or to proclaim to her people, *I am still queen!* Jehu called to her servants to throw her down. Powerless to protect herself, Jezebel fell to her death. Her body became a bloody, trampled heap by the palace wall.

When the men arrived to bury her, all they found were her hands, feet and skull. Elijah spoke the word of God in truth, the dogs had eaten Jezebel's flesh (1 Kings 21:23; 2 Kings 9:26).

Had she lived in the 20th century, Jezebel might have been on the cover of *Time* magazine. She certainly was a woman of impact and power. She was single-minded in her focus, politically correct and confidently self-asserting. She was her own woman and felt free to express her sexuality in her own way. Her husband was also a financial success and leader over whom she had a strong influence.

All the idols in which she had put her confidence, her sensuality, her threats and her power were gone. She left a legacy of murder, sexual immorality and idolatry. Because Jezebel's devotion was not to Almighty God, her unwavering commitment to her gods left her as a *nobody* with *nothing*.

Without Excuse

Jezebel's stubborn rebellion started where most sin begins: pride and ingratitude (Romans 1:21). Like Jezebel, I am a woman without excuse. I have seen the glory of God. I've seen the kingdom spread from a mustard-seed beginning to every continent in the world. I have seen prayers answered, lives changed and illnesses cured. My oldest son and I have been cured of cancer. I have seen God work in the lives of my other two children and my husband. I am loved by them and even better, I am loved *and* redeemed by God. But I still forget to glorify God and be grateful. How *Jezebelious* of me!

When I allow the roots of ingratitude to infiltrate my heart, I focus on the costs of being a disciple. I become blind, deaf and mute to the power and blessings of God. We know every cure has a cost. Am I willing to pay the price?

One of the most personally painful costs I focused on recently was the side-effects of my cancer cure. The immediate treatment for this life-threatening sarcoma was completed in three months, but since this type of cancer feeds on estrogen, I will remain on an estrogen suppressant for the rest of my life.

The loss of estrogen brings with it a set of problems, one being a tendency toward depression. But because of the severe and prolonged nature of my depression, the doctors did not attribute it solely to the loss of estrogen.   At first, I dealt with it as I had my previous down times: I prayed, set my heart and mind to be godly, and relied on God's Spirit to give me joy. After five years of having to wake up and daily decide to be happy, I grew weary of the battle. I was losing my gratitude for life because the daily depression began to seem unbearable. I had known the type of depression that one can *repent out of*, but this was different. Finally, a Christian psychologist suggested that I explore a physical reason for the depression. A genetic disorder was discovered that, praise God, was treatable. The long depression was over!

The next several months were fun and exciting for me. I wanted to make up for all the fun and energy I had missed. In my rush to enjoy life, I was blind to the fact that I had not dealt with the root of ingratitude and with a grudge that I had held against God. In my pride, I laid down the trusty weapons of prayer and reliance on God and replaced them with self-reliance and self-gratification.

Depression hit again. This time it was the kind born out of self-pity, guilt and humanism. It was scary to see how I had become like Jezebel. I too had become blind, deaf, speechless and spiritually dead. Praise God that this kind of depression can be repented out of when it is seen. The victorious deaths of three godly friends helped me to see that I was not ready to face death—a fact that jarred me back to spiritual reality. Remembering the cross and the incredible cost to God and his Son made me deeply penitent and grateful that God's focus was on my cure and not the personal cost to him.

I can be grateful for anything God allows in my life, even cancer or depression, if I use it as an opportunity to draw closer to God. Jezebel had many opportunities to see God and turn to him. She made the wrong choice, again and again. It's a daily decision to keep surrendered to God and to be grateful, but by making that decision, I find joy and leave a living legacy of faith.

Marcia Lamb
Acton, Massachusetts

 FOCUS How do you respond to the costs that come along with the "cure" of Calvary? Which is most difficult for you?

22

SHUNAMMITE WOMAN

IN HIS HANDS

2 Kings 4:8-37, 8:1-6

The miracles performed by the prophets were signs for desperate times. These men were sent by God to beg his people to repent. The miracles performed were confirmation that they represented a powerful God. Israel had long since abandoned the worship of Jehovah for the worship of idols when Elisha came on the scene around 850 B.C., just after the reign of Ahab.

Fascination with superstition and the magic arts had replaced legitimate awe for the one true God. The people's concept of God was distant and fuzzy, as truth mixed with fiction. They were in a self-destruct mode, and their hope for salvation lay in a national, clear-minded, single-hearted return to God. So God unleashed his power through his prophets.

Many of the miracles of the prophet Elisha were compassionate and benevolent. One of his miracles was a reward for the kindness of a generous woman in Shunem.◆

As she arranged the straw inside the bedsack for the new bed, she looked around the room, pleased with the white walls, shaded from the hot sun by the grape arbor over the window. Anticipating the man of God's response, she knew he would be pleased with the table and chair, a quiet place to write and reflect. She recalled the many times Elisha had joined her and her husband for roast lamb and rice and how inspired she was by the accounts of his encounters with the king, his tales of Elijah and the faith he held in his heart for Jehovah God. She felt so pleased that he would choose her house as a haven from the heat on the way from Mt. Carmel to the Jordan River. Her husband had graciously agreed to build this little room as Elisha's retreat. She was happy to serve the prophet in return for all the wisdom and excitement he had brought to her life.

A Dream Come True

Isolated from her family, she sometimes was lonely. Although her husband had provided a comfortable farm for her when they married, she missed the fun of being around people her age. She had eagerly tackled managing her home and the servants, and eventually she began to help her husband to harvest and market the grain and almonds more efficiently. Yes, they had done especially well, since she had contracted with the merchant in Jezreel instead of selling at the local market. She was indeed busy, but she longed for something else. Her husband had given her everything she needed, had made her feel loved and had allowed her to pursue projects; but she had a hidden hope. Oh, to have a child. A son. But she was afraid to dream and her husband was so much older. She should be content.

But then came the promise and prediction from Elisha. *Is it possible that more than 10 months had passed since Elisha told me that I would bear a son? How did he know that I longed for a baby?* As she rested from her chores, short of breath and feeling sluggish from the extra weight she was carrying in her womb, she remembered again the joy mixed with fear she felt when Elisha said she would have a son. Her life had been so predictable. Perhaps that is what had drawn her to Elisha. He never knew the next day's challenges, yet he was certain and secure in allowing his God to direct his life. It made her feel so helpless to realize that Elisha had predicted this accurately. *How could this be happening to me? Who is Jehovah God?*

The promise fulfilled, she cradled her child in her arms. Alarmed by his shallow breathing, she shook him lightly to make sure he was alive. She smiled at herself and her first-baby anxiety, and placed him in his bed.

Lost and Regained

Several years later, her son ran to his father crying, "My head! My head!" After the servant brought him to her, she held him in her lap, comforting him. This time his breathing did stop. He was dead.

What shall I do? My son, my life, has died in my arms. Elisha gave him to me, then took him back, she thought as she laid him on the prophet's bed. *Why did he let this happen? It would have been better if he had not raised my hopes, not given me my dream, than to fulfill it and then shatter it. It hurts so much...but I can endure this. I'm strong. My husband is consumed with the harvest. I'll find Elisha myself; he will have to make the pain go away. Other women have lost their children; surely I can handle this.*

A hurried trip and a miracle of God. Wonder of wonders! She once again held him in her arms, alive and breathing. The man of God had raised him from the dead. A dream twice fulfilled. The woman from Shunem understood more than ever that God is in control. Everything truly is in his hands.

Then Elisha predicted a seven-year famine. He warned her to leave her house and land and go where she would be able to find food. She may have had doubts: *It is hard to walk away from our home when I consider all the labor that we both have put into cultivating the fields and orchards. Someone will move in and take over the farm. How can we leave?* Doubts or not, she obeyed without question because she trusted God *and* his man.

The Vulnerability of Dreaming

This woman was wealthy, confident, in charge of her life. She had a husband who had probably waited to marry, anticipating the responsibilities ahead and who had worked hard to accumulate and cultivate his property. In many ways she was secure, that is why she could be hospitable and work hard to do for others. She was content, not responding to Elisha's offer to reward her kindness. Accepting it would have put her in an awkward position, one of indebting herself to him. Did that fear rise within her when Elisha predicted the arrival of her son? To dream was to give over control to something beyond her. Perhaps she was afraid to hope, to let those close to her see or feel her emotional needs. This could certainly have prompted her to lay her dead son on the bed, to hide his death from her husband, and to say only that she was going to visit the man of God.

She was a determined woman. With the same spirit that she took charge of her life, she pursued Elisha and his faith. The birth of her son solidified her trust in Elisha, and her son's death sent her to Elisha's feet. When God showed her that she was not in control, she knew where to go for help, and God rewarded her faith.

Choose to Dream

Being hospitable, entertaining friends and strangers makes my heart happy. Using my talents to serve others gives me satisfaction. I love to fix problems, organize projects and find the quickest and cheapest way to accomplish the task at hand. There is a blank space in my nature which is filled by these pursuits, and I suspect it is marked "self esteem." Solving dilemmas is a challenge, a way to test my mettle, and it is much more easily accomplished if I can make the decisions and direct the process. This sacrifice of serving can easily become a means of controlling.

The Shunammite woman was content to serve Elisha. But when Elisha gave back, he disturbed her contentment—not just because she had no choice in accepting the gift, but also because he exposed the dream in her heart. This was not a dream like building the room for Elisha or anything she could set out to complete. But this was a dream in God's sphere, one only he could bring about. It took away any ability she had to determine events.

Every January when the topic of resolutions comes up, I am forced to think about my goals for the coming year, something I resist doing. When I allow myself to imagine what God might envision for my life, it's frightening, because I know I am not capable, of making it happen. This year, however, I began to realize that my reluctance to dream had hurt the women I lead. My example of giving in to the comfort of being in control, because I didn't step out past the edge of experience, spoke to the women around me. I subtly showed them that they could stagnate or just be led by circumstances or the decisions of others.

These thoughts came into sharp focus one day when I participated in a group exercise to write an imaginary front page newspaper article on what I would be doing four years from now. My reactions were: *What if I put down something that is totally unrealistic? What if my dream doesn't come true? Or what if I can't even think of an appropriate dream? This is too hard!* I realized that the only future I could envision was the one I could define; I could not imagine one that God could make happen, an impossible one.

When her son was restored, the Shunammite woman learned to dream. Dreaming is hard for me because it means that I must expose my heart, my hopes, needs and longings. When I choose to expose my heart, it is a decision to give over my ability to predict the relationship, to lead the conversation, or to control the future. It means that I express my heart and allow God to determine the outcome. When I admit my need, I give to others in the deepest way, God's way. Somehow my transparency fills a need in others.

Dreaming the impossible is being transparent before God. When I tell God what hurts, what I hope for, what my longings are, he is closer to me.

Expressing my need to him allows him to fill the empty space. If he has filled the space, it stays filled, no matter what happens in my life. This makes me eager to tell others about what God has done and what he will do.

Betty Morehead
Bedford, Massachusetts

 FOCUS

Are you willing to be vulnerable with others?
How open are you about your needs, desires and dreams?
What causes you to hold back?

23

NAAMAN'S SERVANT GIRL

BIG FAITH IN A LITTLE PACKAGE

2 Kings 5:2-19

These were not happy times in Israel. The kingdom had been divided for a century, and the borders of the northern kingdom were being progressively pushed back by Syrian aggression. It was not that God was unable to protect his people's possession, but they had abandoned him so long ago that he now left them to fight their own battles. The promised land, one section at a time, was falling to foreign ownership; the people of Israel were becoming slaves to other nations. But God was still actively demonstrating his power to Hebrew and Gentile alike.

The Syrian army was led by a commander who happened to be a leper. Leprosy was the most dreaded disease of the day. It was incurable and resulted in horrible disfigurement.

The Law God had given his people through Moses was not limited to moral injunctions. God also included health laws that set Israel apart from every other nation in hygiene, diet and disease control. Segregation of lepers was unique to the Hebrews. Other nations, totally ignorant of disease prevention, had situations like Namaan's. He was married and lived with his family. He performed the duties of his job in close contact with his men. He had no concept of contagion and no hope of cure, until he was approached by his wife's little servant girl who knew of a healer in Israel.◆

Sometimes in Biblical history the smallest acts by the most insignificant people affected great changes. This was the case with Naaman's servant girl. We know very little about her. We don't even know her name. We do know that she was an Israelite who had been taken captive by raiding bands from Aram (Syria)—apparently a common practice (2 Kings 5:2, 6:8, 6:23). But, of course, what makes her significant to all generations is her great faith in God.

We can only speculate about her background. A young girl would surely have been taken from her family. Whether she witnessed their deaths or was simply kidnapped, we don't know. Whatever the details, we can know that she experienced incredible trauma. Undoubtedly, she left people grieving their loss and wondering what happened to her. She would have been among others who were also ripped from their homes, families, friends, familiar surroundings and forced to be slaves in a foreign, pagan country.

Chosen by God

This little girl was chosen by God. He had a purpose for her life—a purpose that was not dependent on position, age, background or education. It only depended on her faith. In a time when Israel was very susceptible to foreign, idolatrous influences, a young girl remembered her faith and her God. How tempting it might have been to be bitter, to question a God who would allow her as a child to be taken away from her family to live in a foreign country for the rest of her life. But she did not give in to bitterness or to doubt. When she realized that her master, Naaman, had leprosy, she said to her mistress, "If only my master would see the prophet who is in Samaria! He would cure him of his leprosy" (2 Kings 5:3). She pointed her master to the prophet of the true living God. Because of her faith, Naaman came to this conclusion after his healing: "'Now I know that there is no God in all the world except in Israel'" (2 Kings 5:15). This was a man who was on speaking terms with the pagan king of Syria (Aram). Her faith ultimately reached out to this Syrian king who terrorized the king of Israel. She became a pawn who affected the moves of kings.

God was in control. It was no coincidence that this little girl became a servant to Naaman's wife. God does determine the times and places for people to live in order to seek him (Acts 17:26-27). She could have become anyone's slave, but God placed her where she would have the greatest impact for the kingdom.

Solution-Oriented

This girl must have been a devoted servant. She was a slave who really cared about her master, doing her duty without a sense of drudgery. She easily could have fallen into self pity, into unproductive dreaming about the past and what her life might have been. She could have wished for divine retribution on her captors. But she was different. Seeing the distress of her mistress, her heart was filled with compassion. She wanted to help.

As a young slave, she was quite bold to give advice to her mistress, to presume that she knew more and had something to offer. Her love for her master must have motivated her to speak up and not give in to insecurity. The Bible records only two sentences by this girl, but they are filled with conviction, faith and certainty. She was so confident of the prophet's power that she convinced her mistress, who then, in turn, was able to convince her husband, who then convinced the king. This girl spoke with her child's faith, "He *would* cure him." She did not doubt or think of all the reasons it would not work.

In Luke 4:27 Jesus tells us, "And there were many in Israel with leprosy in the time of Elisha the prophet, yet not one of them was cleansed—only Naaman the Syrian." Naaman, the foreigner and the enemy. What lunacy—the commander of the Syrian army was asking for a favor. In fact, when the king of Israel read the letter from the king of Syria demanding that Naaman be cured, he believed that it was a provocation to war. Relations were not good between these two countries. Not only that, but Naaman was going to humbly request a favor from Elisha the prophet, who was to become a goad in the side of the king of Syria. A foreigner and an enemy was to be the only one that Elisha would ever cure of leprosy because a young girl took her faith with her into a foreign land.

This young slave girl, by her faith and boldness for God, had an impact on the commander of an enemy army, two kings and a prophet. She is an outstanding example of great faith. No matter who we are or how unimportant our role may seem, God will use us to further his kingdom. It depends solely on our faith.

No Shrinking Back

How often I have held back in my life. How often I have wondered if God had made a huge mistake by giving me some particular responsibility. The faith of this young girl inspired me to consider my own lack of faith and my insecurity with God.

I struggle with believing that God has chosen me to make a significant impact. In considering my life, I often see the cup as half empty and not half full. I easily become aware of my own inadequacies and lose sight of the all-powerful, all-knowing God. It is a subtle pride in me that thinks God doesn't really know what he is doing. I think I know better than

God—I know myself and my capabilities. This prideful attitude causes me to hold back—in sharing my faith, in giving advice to people I respect, and even in making bold requests of God.

I have seen how my faithlessness hurts those around me. There is nothing worse than a leader who will not courageously go out in front and lead. If this girl had held back, Naaman would never have been cured. We would never have heard of her or been inspired to imitate her faith. She caused two nations to be confronted by the power of Jehovah God. I am sure the news of Naaman's healing spread like wildfire throughout Israel and Syria.

When I am faithless, people stay in their sin without hope of a cure. I understand clearly from this girl that I never have an excuse for "shrinking back." I have a mission, and I know the "great physician" who is able to heal all hearts and has the cure for death. I am inspired to have greater faith to let God use my life with anyone he chooses. Because after all, he did choose me! And he always does know what he is doing!

Terrie Fontenot
Sydney, Australia

FOCUS

Are you expecting God to do great things with your life? If not, why not?

24

ESTHER

FOR SUCH A TIME AS THIS

Book of Esther

Israel had been split into two kingdoms, and the northern kingdom had long since lost its identity. The people had severed their connection to the God who had made every effort to nurture and bless them. One hundred years after the northern kingdom's fall to Assyria, the southern kingdom, Judah, fell to the Babylonians. Consequently, the Jews lost their national identity and all but a remnant were exiled to Babylon—displaced because of their own unfaithfulness.

For 70 years the Jews lived relatively normal lives in Babylon. Most held onto their beliefs and were faithful to God in a foreign culture.

When the Medes and Persians divided the Babylonian Empire, many of the Jews returned to their homeland to rebuild Jerusalem and to reestablish their nation. Others stayed and worshipped God in synagogues, subject to a succession of Persian kings.

When Xerxes was on the throne, he became displeased with his wife's disobedience (Esther 1:12). This powerful ruler began the search to replace her, little knowing that the *all-powerful* ruler had already selected and carefully prepared his queen's replacement. Her name was Esther.◆

For twelve months she waited. Twelve months to prepare for a date with the king. The lovely and soft Esther was made even more beautiful with six months of oil and myrrh and six months of spices and cosmetics (2:12)...the beauty treatment that might determine the course of her life!

We can only imagine what passed through her mind during this time of waiting. Perhaps she thought back often and fondly to her older cousin Mordecai. He had raised her since the death of her parents, and had brought her up to be respectful, obedient, discreet; to be teachable and to take direction well. Maybe, when he brought her to the palace, he had reminded her to be good and to listen well to Hegai, who was in charge of the women (2:8).

Esther probably nodded, trembling as she left him in the courtyard and walked in with the other maidens. And now, would she be the one who would please the temperamental king? Would she go to his bed only to be discarded to the king's harem along with the other beautiful but rejected women? Or would she be the one to wear the crown?

The Choice

Time passed, each day a reminder to Esther that the outcome of her life rested in the hands of other people. Mordecai had raised her here in Susa, the capital of Persia. Now Hegai controlled her daily allotment of food and her beautification, and soon the king himself would decide her future. More than ever, Esther felt the impact of being a woman who lived by the whims of the men in her life!

Surely she heard the gossip and giggles of the other girls about this King Xerxes: Impulsive and tempestuous, he had already deposed at least one queen. There were plenty of women at his disposal, concubines and "lesser wives." His wish was anyone's command, although his power had caused him much grief already—his marital life as well as his recent military battles in Salamis and Plataea had been utter failures. And yet, he was king, and Esther learned that even if she was to become the queen, she would always have to be on her guard, watching over her shoulder for another egocentric, irrational edict.

Therefore, Esther submitted willingly to the recommendations of Hegai (2:10, 20). She understood that he knew better than anyone what the king wanted in a woman: what colors, what fabrics, what perfumes. And when it was her turn to go to the king, she obeyed Hegai implicitly. Natural beauty and meekness were her strengths, and she used them to the full.

She may have been as surprised as anyone by the king's treatment of her: His kindness and tenderness were the prelude to his choice of her as his queen. Esther, the young, pretty Jewish girl was now queen over an entire kingdom. More feasts and parties; even a holiday named after her! (2:17,18). Yet her life was still lived as an ornament for the king. She had no real power, no true influence in Susa. Her mission in life was to simply wait in her "ivory tower" for the next time her husband would call for her.

The Edict

Esther never forgot her roots, nor did she neglect her relationship with Mordecai. Pampered and protected, she received the news one day from her maids and eunuchs that Mordecai was outside the king's gates, dressed in a goat's hair garment and throwing ashes on himself as he wailed loudly and bitterly. Aghast, Esther tried to solve his problems by sending out some new clothes for him! When Mordecai refused this offer of a temporary solution, Esther summoned her attendant, Hathach (4:1-5).

"Go to Mordecai," she ordered. "Find out what is wrong with him, and why he is behaving this way!" Esther waited, pacing the floor, not realizing that the whole city of Susa was puzzling over an edict from the king about which she, his own wife, had no clue.

When Hathach returned, he carried with him a letter, sealed with the king's signet ring (4:8, 9). But the script meant little to her. Esther had been trained in the womanly arts: sewing, painting and cosmetics. Those were what her time and culture demanded of her. Reading and writing were not high on the list of necessary skills for ladies in her position. Hathach had to patiently explain to the beautiful, illiterate, oblivious queen all the details of the king's edict.

Esther listened in horror: Haman, a snake of a man in high position in the kingdom, had schemed a plan of destruction for the Jewish people, even offering 10,000 talents of silver for their complete annihilation (3:9). The news became even more disgusting when Hathach related to Esther Haman's personal grudge against Mordecai, leading to his vengeance against all his people. But then came the most horrible news of all: "Mordecai wants you to go before the king." Hathach spoke clearly, purposefully. "You are to implore his favor and plead with him for your people."

The Request
Esther's eyes widened in amazement. "But what about the law?" she asked. "You know, the law that says that no one can go before the king without being summoned! And the king has not called for me for a month! Please, Hathach, tell Mordecai that I'm sorry, but I'm afraid that I'm of little use here" (4:10, 11).

Esther's insides were churning as Hathach walked away. Feelings of guilt, followed by rationalizations, alternated back and forth in her mind. No one knew she was a Jew; the question had never been asked. But was she even safe herself? And even if she was, she loved her people, her heritage, her God. But what could she do, anyway? Her beauty had gotten her into the palace, but it did not equip her for political persuasion. The conflicting emotions, as well as the fears, kept her in turmoil until Hathach's return.

Mordecai's words, spoken through Hathach, brought his second and final appeal: "Do not think that because you in the king's house you alone of the Jews will escape. For if you remain silent at this time, relief and deliverance will arise for the Jews from another place, but you and your father's house will perish. And who knows but that you have come to royal position for such a time as this?" (4:13, 14).

A sense of calm passed over Esther as she heard these words. She was needed. God had a plan for her life. Her purposeless, pretty existence now had a meaning of more worth than a thousand outfits of silks and satins, of more worth than all the choice food and luxurious surroundings and the maids who would come running at the clap of her hands. She had been given something to do that could change lives forever, and by the grace of God she would do it.

Immediately Esther took charge. Hesitance and reluctance gave way to resolve and planning. No more questions, no more excuses. She gave the order to Mordecai, through Hathach: "Go, gather together all the Jews who are in Susa, and fast for me. Do not eat or drink for three days, night or day. I and my maids will fast as you do. When this is done, I will go to the king, even though it is against the law. And if I perish, I perish" (4:16).

Esther had to avoid the temptation to rush immediately in to the king and "give him a piece of her mind." She knew this man well, and she knew what she must do to win his favor one more time. She had learned all that before. Besides, she needed the three days. Three days to pray and to rely on God, her greatest security. Three days to draw strength from her maids who loyally fasted with her.

When the three days ended, Esther again wore his favorite colors, fabrics and perfumes. She approached the king with her head held high. Whether she was sent to her death or not, she knew she was doing the right thing, the noble thing. The beauty queen had become a true woman of God.

As he sat on his throne busying himself with his royal responsibilities, King Xerxes looked up and saw this lovely vision. She had captivated his heart, but now his heart had become so heavy with affairs of the kingdom that he had all but forgotten her. He held out his gold scepter, a gesture acknowledging that she pleased him and that she could approach. "Now what is your petition? It will be given to you. And what is your request? Even up to half the kingdom, it will be granted" (5:6).

Esther took a deep breath. The capricious Xerxes could not be taken at face value. She must stick to the plan, to what God had made clear to her. "My petition and my request is this: If the king regards me with favor and if it pleases the king to grant my request, let the king and Haman come tomorrow to the banquet I will prepare for them. Then I will answer the king's question."(5:7-8) This invitation ultimately led to the disclosure of Esther's nationality and to the revealing of Haman's true intentions. The enlightened king was infuriated and immediately ordered the execution of the wicked Haman.

The Result

The course of events that followed changed the course of history for the Jewish nation. Through Esther's influence, a new decree was given that allowed the Jews the right to assemble and protect themselves, and to destroy their enemies (8:11). One woman's altruistic act led to the salvation of many.

Esther's life and actions remind us that God always gives us what we need to accomplish his will for our lives. Esther was a natural beauty, but that was, in itself, a gift from God. She was meek and obedient; God had ingrained that in her from childhood through her upbringing with Mordecai. Her bravery, however, was something she had to struggle to obtain. Courage can only come about when there is true fear. Only when her very life was threatened was Esther able to work through the emotions and make the decision to trust in her God. The worst possible circumstances brought out the best possible woman.

The queen of the Medo-Persian Empire went from a life of ease to a life of impact. Esther had not been a woman who aspired to "change the world;" on the contrary, she desired security. That all changed because she saw a need, and realized that she was the woman to meet that need. Only with that deep conviction was she able to risk her life. Centuries later, she is still the example of a woman who put aside her comfort to take a stand. To be like Esther, we must, as Christian women, realize that God has brought us into his kingdom "for such a time as this." We must use our natural gifts to glorify him, and call on God to change us when life's circumstances call for change. Now is the time to lay down our lives and make an impact in the kingdom of God.

Risk It in Faith

The excuses and rationalizations that I can come up with to get out of a responsibility are many: "It's too hard." "Someone else could do better." "What if I fail?" There are voices in my head trying to convince me that it's okay to give in to my fears and my laziness. Thankfully, God's voice looms larger through his word and reminds me: There's a need, and I'm with you, so just do it!

I was never a woman who wanted to do noble things or change the world. Growing up, my ambition was to live a comfortable life—no risks required. I had it all planned out and could see clearly where I was going each step of the way. I even had some natural talents and abilities that would help me to accomplish this goal.

Then, WHAM! God came into my life (although unknown to me, he had been leading me all along) and turned it all upside down! Suddenly, I had to change everything: my way of thinking, my plans, my dreams, my security...I had to start to live by FAITH! Faith meant accepting God's control of my life. It meant taking risks. It meant stepping out where I couldn't see.

Do you think that only happened when I first became a Christian, and now, after so many years, my life as a disciple has become comfortable and predictable? BY NO MEANS! Constantly, God is putting me in situations where I must face a task or responsibility that requires a stretching of who I am...or who I think I am. And then those old doubts and excuses come along, clamoring to stop me from answering God's call to do the right thing.

If I could present the attitudes that motivate me to take the risks of the Christian life, they would include this: "God has called me to his kingdom for such a time as this." In other words, I see the need, I'm convinced that God wants to use me to meet this need, and therefore, I must do it. My courage, like Esther's, is fueled by the fact that I can make an impact for God and for his kingdom.

My decision that I will take a stand for God continues to lead me down unknown paths. My life is, indeed, an adventure. With each adventure, God is molding my character to have the Christ-like qualities of love, bravery, strength, patience...the list will grow as I accept each new challenge. It's thrilling to be able to live a life that can make an eternal impact on others. Just as God was with Esther, he is with me, leading me, changing me, and giving me the victory!

Kay McKean
Lexington, Massachusetts

 Consider some of the difficult and tumultuous times in your life. Did these circumstances bring out the best in you or the worst? What godly qualities did God bring about because of these times that otherwise would have remained dormant within you?

BIBLIOGRAPHY

Deen, Edith. *All of the Women of the Bible.* New York: Harper and Roe Publishers, 1955.

Halley, Henry H. *Halley's Bible Handbook.* Grand Rapids, Michigan: Zondervan Publishing House, 1965.

Lockyer, Dr. Herbert. *All the Women of the Bible.* Grand Rapids, Michigan: Zondervan Publishing House, 1958.

Lofts, Norah. *Women in the Old Testament.* New York: The McMillan Company, 1949.

Smith, William. *Smith's Old Testament History, revised by Wilbur Fields.* Joplin, Missouri: College Press, 1970.

APPLICATION

1–Eve

1. In adversity, do you grow closer to God in faith and dependence, or do you struggle with doubt, anger or self pity?

2. Do you tend to block out thinking about the negative consequences of sin or do you allow them to motivate you to fight harder against sin?

3. What sins of the heart can be defeated by gratitude?

4. Do you ever block out an awareness of the presence of God? What causes you to do this?

2–Sarah

1. Describe a situation in your life when God called you to go beyond your comfort level. How did you respond, and what were the results?

2. If you are married, how committed are you to pleasing your husband and meeting his needs?

3. Lynn describes submission as "putting someone else's needs ahead of your own." How is this true in various relationships in your life?

4. Has there ever been a time when you lost faith in God's promises? How do you respond when that happens? What do you specifically remind yourself of to help you reclaim your faith?

5. What in Sarah's life encourages you the most?

3-Hagar

1. In what area is God calling you to be submissive to him and to others? How will you respond to that call?

2. What is your view of submission? What passages will help you to have God's view?

3. How do you handle conflict?

4. Who in your life truly knows you?

5. How do you respond when you are treated unfairly?

4-Lot's Wife

1. How intensely do you let your husband's strengths influence you? Why? Why not?

2. Do you fret over your husband's weaknesses and/or allow them to make you lose respect for him? What heart sins must you repent of in order to change this?

3. What things can make you want others to "leave you alone"?

4. What things in your life tempt you to look back?

5. What scriptures give you encouragement to keep looking ahead?

5-Rebekah

1.   How does it affect you when you, like Abraham's servant, witness the specific answer to a prayer?

2.   Once it was clear to Rebekah that it was God's will for her to leave her family to marry Isaac, she quickly obeyed. When are specific times that God has made his will clear to you? How did you respond?

3.   As a mother, teacher or friend, do you show favoritism? What do you believe is the root of this sin?

4.   In what ways are you tempted to manipulate in order to get your way?

5.   Rebekah shows us that we can start in faith and end in defeat. How do you guard against losing your faith?

6-Rachel

1.   Rachel felt inferior because of her inability to have children. She compared herself to Leah and saw that she fell short. In which area have you felt inferior as you compared yourself to others? On the other hand, what are your strengths and talents that could tempt others to feel inferior?

2.   No one of us has all gifts or all talents. Why is this important for us to remember? How does 1 Corinthians 12 (the body, the church) speak to this idea?

3.   When Rachel felt insecure and inferior (lacked faith), how did she respond to her husband? Why do we blame others when we lack faith?

4.   What are we forgetting when we become ungrateful? How can we keep grateful hearts?

5.   When we try to prove to others that we are worthy of their love or their approval, how does it affect our relationships?

7–Potiphar's Wife

1.   How do you respond to a woman who is like Potiphar's wife? Is it hard for you to have compassion or vision for her?

2.   What practical steps must a wife take to stay single-mindedly faithful to her own husband?

3.   How have you responded when you have been in a position like Joseph's and someone has blamed you for their sin?

4.   In what area are you are most vulnerable to the attacks of the roaring lion?

8–Miriam

1.   What life situation has caused you to feel displaced? What emotions did you experience? How did your faith impact you during this time?

2.   What happens in your life when you trust in yourself rather than trusting in God?

3.   What would you say is the root of jealousy? When are you most tempted to be jealous?

4.   Do you ever believe that God cannot use you because you have too many weaknesses? How can Miriam's story encourage you when you have these negative thoughts?

9–Rahab

1. Rahab made a decision of faith over feelings. In what ways must you make faith decisions when your feelings are telling you something different?

2. When your faith grows weak, what *scarlet cord* reminds you of your decision to follow Jesus?

3. Even though she was a pagan prostitute, God used Rahab powerfully to work his will. How should this encourage you when you feel unworthy to be used by God?

4. God sent Rahab an opportunity in the form of two spies—an opportunity to express her faith. What opportunities does God send you in order to test your faith?

5. Though she had only heard of him secondhand, Rahab was awed by the one God of the Israelites. How can you develop your awe and respect for God?

10–Deborah

1. What experiences have you had in calling out desperately to God in a time of great stress? What help or protection did you receive?

2. Share a time when you faced a threat, but had the active support of others. How did the support of others impact your fears?

3. What scriptures have proved to be helpful in your battles against fear? Have you commited any of them to memory? Select some to memorize, and then quote them aloud to begin each day.

4. Do negative circumstances tend to cause you to lose faith in God? Why? What if Deborah had done that? How can you change your way of thinking in this area?

5. How supportive are you of the male leadership in your life?

11-Delilah

1. In what areas does the temptation of self-importance attack you?

2. Have you ever said to a leader, a parent or to your husband, "You just don't love me"? In what ways have you used this statement to manipulate others or to protect yourself?

3. Do you naturally tend toward being a constant drip or a constant encouragement? How do you work on becoming more encouraging?

4. In what ways does Satan try to deceive you through your emotions?

12-Naomi

1. Describe a time when you needed a Ruth in your life to remind you of God's promises.

2. What toll have you seen bitterness take in your life? How determined are you not to allow it to take root in your heart?

3. Even though Naomi had a daughter-in-law who was committed to her, she returned home bitter. What is the relationship between bitterness and ingratitude?

4. What inspires you the most about Irene Gurganus' life?

13–Ruth

1. What circumstances have seemed overwhelming to you? How did you respond to these circumstances? What did you learn from Ruth about responding to difficult circumstances?

2. What about Ruth's character most impresses you? How do you want to become like her in this area?

3. What does Ruth's story tell you about the faithfulness of God?

4. In what areas are you most tempted to give in to your fears? How will you overcome these fears?

14–Hannah

1. If you had been in Hannah's situation, how would you have responded to Peninnah?

2. Are you ever discontent about what you don't have? Does it keep you from appreciating what you do have?

3. Wives can cause their husbands to feel helpless and inadequate by refusing their help or comfort. Elkanah really wanted to encourage his wife, but he could not give her a child. If you are married, do you make it easy for your husband to encourage you, or do you have to get your way before you will be encouraged?

4. Hannah is a great example of pouring out her heart to God. Do you tend to be open and honest with God, or are you distant and impersonal? He longs for closeness with us.

5. Do you pray in faith, believing you are heard, or in doubt, hoping you are heard?

15-Michal

1. In what ways might you tend to focus more on outward appearance than on the heart?

2. Has God ever given you something you wanted with all your heart? Have you ever taken this answer for granted? When this happens, how do you renew your gratitude?

3. Why do you think Michal despised David when she saw him dancing before the ark of God in a linen ephod? Can you think of instances when you have the same type of attitude toward your husband, leaders or other Christians?

4. In what ways do you want to imitate David's spirit before the Lord and others?

5. Michal made some unspiritual choices that hurt her and the people in her life. How can you guard against making unspiritual choices?

16-Abigail

1. How have you responded when your dreams were not fulfilled as you had expected?

2. When your husband or someone else is insensitive to you, how do you respond? Do you lash out, fall into self-pity, deny your resentment or bear with others in love—being honest and forgiving?

3. How do you see tough situations forming the character of Christ in you?

4. Abigail did not hesitate to do what was right and appropriate. How can you prepare yourself to have good judgment quickly in life situations?

17 –Tamar

1.   Where do you turn first when you have been hurt–to a family member, a friend or God?

2.   Is there a painful memory in your heart that has a hold on you? Have you been open about your response to what happened to you or have you simply explained the circumstances?

3.   Tamar made the wrong choice in her situation. Have you made any wrong choices that have allowed evil to have victory over good? What is the first step you must take to change that?

18–Queen of Sheba

1.   How were you affected by your first visit with a group of Christians who were "truly devoted to God"?

2.   For which questions did you seek answers in coming to faith in God? What answers did you find?

3.   The Queen of Sheba was "a woman of passion and a leader by nature." Is this the type of person you naturally are? If yes, how have you learned to humble yourself and trust God in your passion and in your leadership? If no, how have you grown in your fervor and decisiveness since becoming a disciple?

4.   What sins in your life could overcome you and cause you to stop short of victory?

19–Gomer

1. For those who are married:

    a. Are you wisely aware that you could fall into the net of adultery? What precautions do you take in your relationships with men to keep this sin out of your life and your marriage?

    b. Do you find yourself taking your husband for granted? How can you show him how special he is to you?

    c. "Gomer was unsupportive, unreliable and unpredictable." In what areas do you strive to be supportive, reliable and predictable (trustworthy)?

2. Selfishness destroys relationships. Selflessness builds them up. How have others built you up through their selflessness?

3. God is overjoyed with us, his bride, as we are faithful to him. How can you bring God joy today?

20–Widow of Zarephath

1. In what ways has God called you to trust him when you could not see how things would work out?

2. Had Elijah given in to sentimentality, he would have blocked the working of God in this widow's life. Can you think of ways that you justify sentimentality and confuse it with compassion as you seek to meet others' needs?

3. How have you been blessed by putting God's will first in your life?

4. In what ways does the widow of Zarephath take away your excuses for faithlessness?

5. Who are the *Elijahs* God has put in your life? Are you thankful for them?

21-Jezebel

1. Did you relate to Jezebel more than you would have thought? In what ways?

2. Pride is powerful! How have you seen its effects in your life? How do you guard your heart from this deadly sin?

3. "Jezebel obviously gave no honor to God because she had little respect for people created in his image." Who are the people you are specifically called to respect? Do you show honor to God by respecting them?

4. If, indeed, Jezebel was affected by her sin momentarily and if she did give in to tears of remorse, she quickly closed her heart again. Have you ever been in a situation when you almost humbled yourself but stopped short because of your pride?

5. When you are surrendered to God and grateful for his working in your life, how is your joy level affected?

22-Shunammite Woman

1. Are you sometimes afraid to dream? Why?

2. In what ways do you trust in yourself and your own talents and strengths rather than trusting in God?

3. Those of us who are mothers know that some of our greatest fears center around our children and their safety, spiritually and physically. If you are a mother, how are you learning that even with your children, God is in control?

4. What can you learn from this woman about practicing hospitality? (Romans 12:13; 1 Peter 4:9).

5. How does your transparency meet a need in the lives of others?

23-Naaman's Servant Girl

1.   Describe a situation in which you should have spoken up for Jesus, but you did not because you felt intimidated or "out-classed." What does Naaman's servant girl teach you about giving in to these feelings?

2.   Describe a situation in which you followed through boldly even though you felt insecurity (lack of faith)?

3.   This young girl easily could have felt that that life had dealt her an unfair blow. In what ways have you been tempted to feel like a victim? How have you learned that God's grace is sufficient for you?

4.   Do you ever doubt that God can use you? How have you been inspired by this girl to put that thinking to death?

24-Esther

1.   Esther had to make a choice between fear and faith. How do you personally overcome fear with your faith?

2.   "I'm afraid that I'm of little use here." Esther underestimated the impact that she could have. When were some times in your life when you thought you were of little use, but God proved you wrong?

3.   "One woman's altruistic act led to the salvation of many." How can your unselfishness specifically lead to the salvation of others?

4.   How does a close, daily walk with God turn life into an adventure?

COMING: EARLY 1995

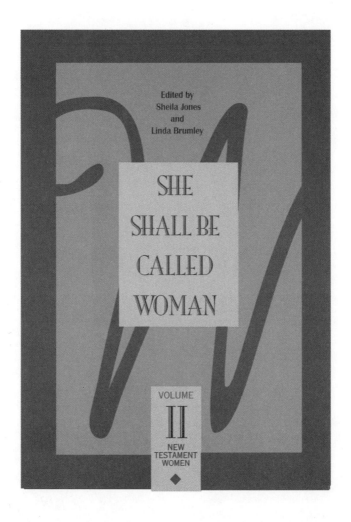

Edited by
Sheila Jones
and
Linda Brumley

SHE
SHALL BE
CALLED
WOMAN

VOLUME
II
NEW
TESTAMENT
WOMEN

You have spent time with women of the Old Testament and those who wrote about them. Soon you will meet women who lived during the first century—along with the present-day writers who, once again, share their own hearts.

**For credit card orders call 1-800-727-8273
or contact your local Christian bookstore.**

Planning a wedding that gives glory to God

Here is a book by disciples for disciples. First, Kay McKean gives you the right spiritual perspective, then Nancy Orr discusses all the details, deadlines and directions.

Included is a three-month-countdown checklist to make sure everything is covered—from wedding invitations to honeymoon reservations.